Date Due

NEW LIFE
IN THE CHURCH

NEW LIFE
IN THE
CHURCH

Robert A. Raines

HARPER & BROTHERS, PUBLISHERS
New York

NEW LIFE IN THE CHURCH

To my father and mother

Contents

Preface   9

I   The Loss of Mission   13

> The Lord . . . set me down in the midst of the valley; it was full of bones. . . . and lo, they were very dry. And he said to me, "Son of man, can these bones live?" —Ezekiel 37:1-3.

II   The Necessity of Conversion   20

> Truly, truly I say to you, unless one is born anew, he cannot see the kingdom of God.—John 3:3.

III   Conversion Begins in Awakening   31

> Awake, O sleeper, and arise from the dead, and Christ shall give you light.—Ephesians 5:14.

IV   Conversion Continues by Decision   38

> And Jesus said to them, "Follow me." . . . And immediately they left their nets and followed him.—Mark 1:17, 18.

V   Conversion Matures by Growth   47

> We are meant to grow up into Christ . . . until we arrive at real maturity, the measure of the stature of the fullness of Christ.—Ephesians 4:13, 15.

VI   Conversion Endures in Discipline   55

> It is for discipline that you have to endure.—Hebrews 12:7.

VII   Conversion Takes Place in Koinonia   65

> And they devoted themselves to the apostles' teaching and fellowship, to the breaking of bread and the prayers. —Acts 2:42.

VIII   The Imperative: Conversion within the Church   73

> For the time has come for judgment to begin with the
> household of God.—I PETER 4:17.

IX   The Strategy: Koinonia Groups   78

> Let us consider how to stir up one another to love and
> good works, not neglecting to meet together, . . . but
> encouraging one another.—HEBREWS 10:24, 25.

X   New Creation in the Church: Changing Lives   88

> Therefore, if any one is in Christ, he is a new creation;
> the old has passed away, behold, the new has come.—II
> CORINTHIANS 5:17.

XI   New Creation in the Church: The Lay Ministry
Emerges   103

> And his gifts were . . . for the equipment of the saints,
> for the work of ministry. . . .—EPHESIANS 4:11–12.

XII   The Recovery of Mission   125

> You shall be my witnesses in Jerusalem . . . and to the
> end of the earth.—ACTS 1:8.

Notes   147

Index   151

Preface

This book was conceived in the fall of 1958 when opportunity was given to make a series of talks at the Indiana Yearly Meeting of Friends on the theme "Conversion within the Church." This material was expanded and prepared in manuscript form during the summer and fall of 1959.

I am not a professional theologian nor a practiced writer. For the errors of interpretation and inadequacies of writing in this book I apologize to the reader. Much of the book was written in the odd moments snatched from a parish minister's schedule.

A special word of appreciation is extended to those who encouraged and assisted me in the preparation of the manuscript:

I am deeply grateful to Elton Trueblood, Professor of Philosophy at Earlham College and a prophet for Christ in our time, who has given me the benefit of his counsel and friendship since my days as an undergraduate at Yale. He suggested that I write this book, encouraged me as it developed, and in reading the manuscript made valuable suggestions which greatly improved it.

My gratitude goes to John Lynn Carr, pastor of Pleasant Hills Methodist Church of Cleveland, Ohio, who carefully read the manuscript, and whose penetrating criticisms resulted in substantial revisions and additions.

I am indebted to Gordon Cosby, pastor of the Church of the Savior in Washington, D.C., in conversation with whom my thought on the mission of the church was sharpened and clarified.

I owe special debts of gratitude to Paul Schubert, Professor of New Testament Criticism and Interpretation at Yale Divinity School, under whose teaching I learned to love the New Testament; to Charles Luckey, pastor of the Middleburgh Heights Community Church of Cleveland, who kept encouraging me to write.

Mrs. Robert Mooney and Mrs. Herman Brown were of invaluable assistance in the painstaking preparation of the manuscript itself.

The good people of Aldersgate Church, Cleveland, first suffered through much of this material as it came to them in the form of sermons. To them, and especially to the people in the *koinonia* groups, in whose fellowship I have learned more about the new life in Christ than from many books on the subject, I owe a debt of abiding gratitude.

This book would not have been possible without the encouragement, assistance, and criticisms offered by my wife, Peggy, whose willingness to forgo many family good times that we might both work on the manuscript is but one expression of her selfless concern for our mutual ministry.

Cleveland, Ohio   ROBERT A. RAINES
October, 1960

NEW LIFE
IN THE CHURCH

I

The Loss of Mission

> The Lord . . . set me down in the midst of the
> valley; it was full of bones. . . . and lo, they were
> very dry. And he said to me, "Son of man, can these
> bones live?"
>
> Ezekiel 37:1–3*

Several years ago Rachel Carson wrote a fascinating book about the ocean, called *The Sea Around Us*. In it she described the microscopic vegetable life of the sea which provides food for many of the ocean's smallest creatures. She told how these little plants drift thousands of miles wherever the currents carry them, with no power or will of their own to direct their own destiny. The plants are named *"plankton,"* a Greek word which means "wandering" or "drifting." Plankton is an accurate term to describe the wandering plant life of the ocean.

Plankton is also an accurate term to describe the people of twentieth-century America. For we have lost our sense of direction; we seem powerless to direct our own destiny; we are without purpose in the world. We have lost our sense of mission. Years ago the poet T. S. Eliot spoke of us when he wrote that we are the hollow men, men whose inner life has withered away, men who have lost their souls. Some of our prophets have been speaking the same word to us in more recent days. The political commentator Walter Lippmann, writing at the time of Nikita Khrushchev's visit to America, said:

The challenge of [Soviet Russia] is aimed directly at the critical weakness of our society. The weakness is that for the time being our

* Except where otherwise noted, Scripture quotations are from the Revised Standard Version.

people do not have great purposes which they are united in wanting to achieve. . . . Thus in our encounter with the Soviet rulers, in the confrontation of the two social orders, the question is whether this country can recover what it does not have—a sense of great purpose and of high destiny.[1]

This national loss of mission is reflected in the formulation of our foreign policy. Max Ways writes in a recent book:

. . . the policy of the United States seems to be swirling into an eddy, a dead end. . . . We will not be able to export the central American Proposition of strong but limited government until we recapture for ourselves a greater measure of its full and intense meaning. We cannot carry a message that we have forgotten.[2]

The loss of mission is reflected in the field of education. The current educational ferment is at root a confusion of basic purpose. We do not know what we want to accomplish in our schools. Therefore, we try to accomplish a little bit of everything. The human result is disturbing. Clifton Fadiman writes in the *Saturday Review:*

The average high school graduate today does not know who he is, where he is, or how he got there. He is lost. By that I mean he feels little relation to the whole world in time and space. He may "succeed," become a law-abiding citizen, etc. . . . yet during most of his life, and particularly after his 40th year or so, he will feel vaguely disconnected, rootless, purposeless. Like the very plague he will shun any searching questions as to his own worth, to his own identity.[3]

We experience the loss of mission in the routinized life of work and community. We feel ourselves to be cogs in the industrial machine by day, and ciphers in the homogenized neighborhood by night. We feel the overwhelming pressures to conform, to lapse into the crowd, to relinquish responsibility, to lose individuality. We let Hollywood or General Motors determine our goals in life. The great symbol of our passivity is the television set, which bombards our senses, dulls our capacity to discriminate, and robs us of our time. We succumb to living with proximate goals as substitutes for abiding purpose. We know pleasure, but seldom joy. We know ease, but rarely peace.

The church too has lost her sense of mission. The church has accommodated herself to the cultural climate. The church is no longer changing culture, but is being changed by culture. The

church is not enabling her people to live with purpose in a world
without purpose. The average church member has little sense of
individual mission in the world. If one were to ask him if he were
a member of a "chosen race, a royal priesthood, a holy nation,"
he would surely reply, "Why no. I'm a member of Main Street
Methodist Church"; or worse, "Why no, I'm a member of Sam
Smith's Church." He wouldn't understand that to be a Christian
means precisely that one is a member of a chosen race, a royal
priesthood, a holy nation. The people believe in God and support
the institution of the church and enter into its activities, but they
do not believe they are chosen to be salt, light, and leaven in the
world. They do not believe they are chosen to be Christ's witnesses in the world. They shrink from the very idea of personal
witness. Their typical response to Christ's summons, "You did
not choose me, but I chose you and appointed you that you
should go and bear fruit . . ." (John 15:16), is: "Here am I,
Lord. Send *him*." They accept the conditions of life in the world
with little thought that these conditions ought to be changed,
and no idea that they as Christians are called to be the agents of
God's reconciling changes.

The loss of mission appears in the local church, which is usually content to grow in physical stature and in favor with its immediate environment. The whole idea of outreach is delegated to
a "Committee On Missions," which concerns itself largely with
the financial support the church gives to foreign and home
agencies of the denomination. This "segregation of concern"
neatly exempts ninety-nine of one hundred people in a church
from a sense of personal responsibility. Thus we lose our individual concern in corporate irresponsibility.

That the average church member and the typical local church
have lost their sense of mission is ultimately a judgment upon us
who are leaders of the church. How tragically we succumb to the
secular pressures upon us. How rapidly we lose our zeal, our sense
of urgency. How easily we accept the pattern imposed upon us
by our culture, so that we accept our *ministry* as a *job*. Pathetically
the church apes the world in assigning authority and financial
reward to its most "successful" men. The power, prestige, and
perquisites the church can bestow upon her leaders too often result in our defensive support of the institution that houses the

church's life, and our blindness to the mission that is the true church. We prostitute our mission to the world by reducing it to keeping pace with the population growth of our community. We externalize our mission so that it becomes wrapped up in statistics and structures. We pose for ourselves numerical goals which become the substitute for our reconciling thrust into the world. Status seeking is no stranger to the church, whose leaders have been called instead to kingdom seeking.

William H. Lazareth, Professor of Systematic Theology at The Lutheran Theology Seminary in Philadelphia, Pennsylvania, pinpointed the church's perennial problem with its own egocentricity:

. . . may I remind you that a church convention is often a particularly tempting place to re-introduce religion into Christianity. Here we can be involved in all kinds of religious "dead works" in our own annual rite of oiling the ecclesiastical machinery:
1) *parliamentary dead works*—in which your political knowledge of Robert's Rules of Order becomes more important than your pastoral knowledge of the Sermon on the Mount;
2) *budgetary dead works*—in which your financial knowledge of amortization becomes more important than your theological knowledge of the pearl of great price; and
3) *statistical dead works*—perhaps the most blasphemous of all today—in which men who go around peddling Jesus like soap, analyze their annual reports as if they were stockholders in Procter and Gamble.

Brothers in Christ, we have been called by God to be faithful priests and not successful salesmen. The "St." before the names of the apostles stands for "saint" and not "statistician." Indeed, it is only because they were saints and not statisticians that they were able to look upon a 5 ft. 10 in., 165-pound, hook-nosed Jew hanging on a cross—and call it a divine victory, rather than a human defeat. (I sometimes wonder what Jesus' annual congregational report would have looked like if he had made one out on Good Friday afternoon. Certainly there would be little there to justify his "promotion" to a growing suburb of Jerusalem, to say nothing of Pittsburgh or New Delhi!)[4]

The church is constantly seeking to save herself, to build herself up in terms of worldly status and power. The church is afraid of her mission, and well she might be. Her mission is to lose her life in the world, that her life and the world's life may be saved. We of the church are guilty. All of us stand under judgment. We have declined the cross which beckons us into a world of suffering, evil, and injustice. We have turned away from reconciling the world, thinking it enough to be reconciled ourselves. In a recent conference on human relations, a church leader was asked what the church ought to do in the problem of race relations. The reply was: "Well, we can't go any faster than our laymen." This appears harmless. But, in fact, it is a way of saying: "If the will of our people and the will of God are in conflict, we shall do the will of the people."

The church becomes the mouthpiece of the people instead of the voice of God. The church, which is meant to be at tension with the customs and traditions of every culture, changes her protective coloring like a chameleon to suit the environment she is in. Indeed, "The time has come for judgment to begin with the household of God" (I Peter 4:17).

And the judgment is clear; the world pays little attention to the church. Russia is able to allow some measure of freedom in the church there because the church has been rendered harmless. The awful truth is that despite all our freedom, the American church seems as powerless to affect American materialism as does the Russian church to influence Russian materialism. The world believes it has tamed and domesticated the church and can keep her busily occupied in cultivating her own garden. The world has pulled the teeth of the church, and no longer listens to her enfeebled message.

Yet God in His mercy will not let us be content in our missionless life. Even in the midst of the church's numerical and financial successes, we feel uneasy, unsatisfied, guilty. In our moments of humility, we know that we are failing, although we do not know why. We want to be used by God in His reconciling work in the world, but we are involved and caught in the purposelessness of our time. We too are being strangled by the cords of our own vested interests, and we struggle in vain to deliver ourselves from this body of death. We know that we are dry bones. We are like the bones which have come together, with sinews on them, and flesh upon them, with skin to cover them, but no breath in them. We are the hollow men. We have the physical equipment, but we lack the Spirit. We hear the Lord's question addressed to us: "Son of man, can these bones live?"

This book is written to share a small but glorious experience in which the dry bones have begun to live. The promise of God is being fulfilled: "I will put my Spirit within you, and you shall live" (Ezekiel 37:14). This is the experience of a local church, and specifically of a rather small number of people in that church. It is no success story because we have only discovered that we had lost our sense of mission, or never had it. We have been lost and are only now being found. We are being released from our bondage to life without mission, released into the Christian freedom of life with mission. We are only at the beginning of our particular mission, on the edge of our ministry to the world. We see in a mirror dimly, but one thing we know—we see! We are mindful of the events in which we have been awakened to our true nature and our real mission. We are grateful to the Holy Spirit for awakening us. We here share our own spiritual pilgrimage in the hope that it may be useful to other churches in the recovery of their mission to the world.

In the last several years a number of people in our church have been rediscovering who they are as Christians and what their mission is. This experience was nothing that any of us planned or even anticipated. It came as a gift, a surprising outcome of meeting together in small groups for Bible study, prayer, and the sharing of experience. We know that these groups have been central to this experience. We know that the study of the New Testament has been at the heart of it. We have watched our friends changing radically and permanently in the context of these groups. We are convinced that real change in ourselves is necessary for the recovery of our mission. We know for ourselves the validity of Paul's declaration: ". . . if any one is in Christ he is a new creation; the old has passed away, behold, the new has come" (II Corinthians 5:17).

The new life has come for many. There is again a stirring in our souls, a warming of our hearts, a stretching of the mind, a new power for our wills. There is rising among us a sense of urgent mission. As we have been rediscovering ourselves, so we are beginning to understand the purpose of our fellowship together.

This life *is* new. It is different from our former life. It is life in the Spirit. It brings forth the desire to serve and witness. Though we are only in the infancy of this new creation, we know that we are being driven on mission into the world. Our future is in the world.

Our past is in the church. It is in the church that God has been making the new creation. The recovery of mission has come out of the new creation. The new creation in the church is the fruit of corporate conversion within the church. For, as we reflect upon these years of our changing lives, we can see that we needed to be changed. We *had* to become new persons. Our old selves simply couldn't and wouldn't go and witness in the world. We have discovered in our own experience the necessity of conversion.

II

The Necessity of Conversion

Truly, truly I say to you, unless one is born anew,
he cannot see the kingdom of God.

John 3:3

Several months ago an unusual luncheon was held in a small
room on the third floor of an unpretentious office building in
Cleveland, Ohio. The room was the office of a man who owns a
chain of drive-in restaurants. There were eight men present, all of
them businessmen of Cleveland, one of them a Negro. This was
a prayer group, which convenes at 12:15 P.M. every Friday in this
place.

One man read aloud a magazine article while the rest of us
ate in silence; chili was the order of the day. After the reading
there was discussion based on its theme, a sharing of personal
experience that was pertinent, and then prayer around the circle.
Precisely at 1:15 P.M. the meeting adjourned and the men returned to their work. It was a most impressive hour, and obviously
an experience and a fellowship to which these men gave unique
priority in their busy schedules.

After the others had gone, the host related how he happened
to become concerned with such a prayer group. Nine years before,
he was getting started in the business world. He had come from
the wrong side of the tracks, had had a rough childhood, and had
to struggle his way up the ladder of success. As an adult he didn't
think twice about the church all year long.

He married. A son was born. As the boy grew older, he and his
wife wondered about Sunday School and religion. One Sunday

he took the boy to Sunday School, and stayed himself for worship.
He was interested. One thing led to another. On one occasion
he heard someone talk about tithing as one of the disciplines of
the Christian life. This was a very practical matter which he
could understand, and he and his wife decided to try it out. Their
interest in the life of the church deepened. Within a matter of
several months they found themselves deeply involved in Christian faith and fellowship. In the course of time, this man felt the
need to go more deeply into the life of prayer, together with other
men. He started a prayer group, which has been meeting regularly
now for eight years in his office.

Recently he came to speak to the men of Aldersgate Church
in Cleveland. He is not a gifted public speaker; his education has
been mainly in the world. He remained seated before the men.
Someone asked a question about his prayer life. In quiet, humble
manner he shared his experience with us. He described the time
when it became possible for him and his wife to pray together,
and what it meant to their marriage. He told us how the prayer
group shored him up and strengthened him. He said, "I am weak;
I would be lost without the fellowship of this group to uphold
me." For the men present it was a deeply moving experience, a
partial result of which was the emergence of three men's prayer
groups in that church. Here is a man who is being converted to
Christ.

What is conversion? What does it mean to be converted to
Christ? The King James Version of the Bible translates the following texts in this fashion:

Acts 3:19   Repent ye therefore, and *be converted*, . . .

Matthew 18:3 . . . except ye *be converted* and become as little chil-
                 dren, ye shall not enter into the kingdom of
                 heaven.

The Revised Standard Version translates these texts:

Acts 3:19   Repent therefore, and *turn again*, . . .

Matthew 18:3 . . . unless you *turn* and become like children, you
                 will never enter the kingdom of heaven.*

*Italics mine.

This turning or being turned is not merely a change of physical direction. It is a purposive change, a stopping in one's tracks, a giving of all of one's attention to a person or situation that up to that moment had not claimed it.[1] Alfred Kazin, editor and author, in an article describing the revolutionary impact of Sigmund Freud on the world, has put in concise terms the nature of such change:

The only kind of change in life which means anything because it transforms everything in its path, is that which changes peoples' thinking, their deepest convictions, that which makes them see the world in a different way. This doesn't happen often.[2]

In specifically Christian perspective, such change describes the encounter in which a person is given new life by God in Christ. One Sunday morning several years ago, a young woman, her husband, and their three children were baptized. This couple helped start a Bible Study Group in whose fellowship they were turned by God to Christ. Three years later she wrote a letter in which she said:

I have been searching my own heart to understand all that has happened to me during the past three years. I have wondered who I am, and why I am, and where I am going. Of course I don't yet know all the answers, but through prayer and Bible study I can see the fog beginning to lift and disappear. As I look back beyond these last three years I am surprised and bewildered, because all events are so hazy, and I myself, as I was then, I barely recognize. Through God's grace which has been given to me, I see that all that is past is dim, because it was not until three years ago when you introduced me to Jesus Christ that I began to live. I have had many periods of turbulence and depression, and I know that I will have more, owing to my human nature. But through God's grace I am stopped and pulled up again. I can never sink too far; I can never turn back, because God has made me a new creature in Christ through the gift of His son.

This is one person's understanding of what it means to be converted to Christ—a conversion in which there is a beginning but no ending; a conversion in which there are both crisis and process, in which one is constantly by grace through faith *becoming* a Christian.

Many people have been brought up in what we like to call the "liberal" tradition of Protestantism; and a great tradition it is. It labored painfully through the seeming conflicts of science and religion a generation ago; it brought us through troubled waters into a time when we can approach the Bible with the tools of historical and literary analysis as well as in faith; it pioneered the humane movements in social and industrial relations. We are all in debt to the liberal tradition.

But liberal Protestantism has left the field of conversion to the Fundamentalists. We have neglected the central mission of the church, which is to go and make disciples, in favor of the easier and more congenial task of nurturing church members. We have not expected lives radically to be changed; we have been content with ourselves as we are and others as they are; we have tried to live by allegiance to the Father and respect for Jesus, but without the Holy Spirit. We have taken refuge in the staid, comfortable, totally unbiblical notion of what may be called *osmosis Christianity*. This is the optimistic assumption that people soak up Christian faith by being reared in a Christian home or by spending enough hours in the atmosphere of the church—the idea that we get onto the heaven-bound escalator in the cradle room, and more or less inevitably are landed on the top floor of the building, which is heaven. This is something like the process of enrolling a newborn child in a fashionable preparatory school, guaranteeing his entrance there years hence.

So it is that our churches are crowded with honest, genial folk who stopped going to Sunday School when they were ten years of age, and thus have a foggy, halo-ridden picture of a Jesus preoccupied with lambs: folk who were swept into church membership around the age of twelve because it was the thing all the other children were doing, folk who perhaps never once have been challenged to make an adult commitment of life to Christ, with all its implications.

For the New Testament doctrine is not "justification by osmosis," but "justification by faith." The faith of our fathers makes no difference in our lives until it becomes our faith. The faith of the church must be appropriated, personally received and entered into, if we are to be converted, if our lives are to continue being changed by Christ. And this is no side issue, no optional matter of individual whim or fancy. Jesus said to Nicodemus,

"You must be born anew. . . . unless one is born anew he cannot see the kingdom of God." Nothing ambiguous or foggy or tentative about that, is there? You *must* be born anew, you *must* be converted. Jesus didn't say, "Nicodemus, I think it might be a pretty good idea sometime for you to consider the possibility of perhaps under the right circumstances, when you feel like it, being born anew." No, Jesus talked to Nicodemus about *the necessity of conversion.*

Let us be clear that we are dealing here with no isolated or unrepresentative text of the New Testament. The whole gospel is the good news about new life in Christ. The language describing the new life is rich and varied.

. . . repent* and believe in the gospel (Mark 1:15).

. . . unless you turn and become like children, you will never enter the kingdom of heaven (Matthew 18:3).

. . . unless one is born anew, he cannot see the kingdom of God (John 3:3).

. . . we have been born anew to a living hope . . . (I Peter 1:3).

We know that we have passed out of death into life . . . (I John 3:14).

. . . if anyone is in Christ, he is a new creation; the old has passed away, behold, the new has come (II Corinthians 5:17).

The point is that however one describes it, conversion from the old way of life to the new is the heart of the New Testament.

Jesus talked to Nicodemus about the necessity of conversion. His words have striking, brutal relevance to the modern church. Let us consider this fascinating interview between Jesus and Nicodemus. We know something about Nicodemus, enough to know that he was a fine person, of impeccable character, just the sort of man to be chairman of the Board of Trustees or lay leader of the local church. He might have been either in his synagogue, for he was a Pharisee—a leader of the religious community of his day, a person who undertook special self-disciplines in order to grow in his relationship with God. Nicodemus was also a ruler of the Jews, which meant that he had achieved some civic and

*The word "repent" means to have a complete change of mind and being.

perhaps political power and recognition. Later on in the Gospel according to John we discover that Nicodemus defended Jesus when Jesus was attacked by Jewish leaders; and at the end Nicodemus was there to help Joseph of Arimathea care for the body of Jesus after the crucifixion. One of the most appealing men in all the New Testament is Nicodemus. To such a man, Jesus talked of the need of conversion.

Nicodemus must have thought to himself, "Why do I need to be converted? I believe in God; I work harder than most people to do God's will. What's the matter with my present life? I'm a good man, a good husband, a good churchman. I treat everybody right. Born anew, start all over again, be given a new life? Why is conversion necessary?"

Conversion is necessary because sin is real. The fact that one grows up in the church, acknowledges the Ten Commandments, tries to live by what he calls "Christian principles," obeys the Golden Rule, doesn't alter the fact that he is a sinner. The story of Adam is the story of every man. Every man puts himself at the center of the world. Every man is bent inward. By nature every man seeks his own will. This is deeply rooted in him and cannot be educated out of him or psychoanalyzed out of him. Human nature cannot change by itself or be changed by any human agency. Sin means that our reason is warped by our pride, so that we can have only partial vision of truth. Sin means that our heart is cooled by our selfishness, so that we cannot make ourselves love our enemies. Sin means that our will is captive to our desires, so that we are unable by ourselves to do God's will. If God helps only those who are able to help themselves, then we are lost. For in the deepest sense, we cannot help ourselves. "Who will deliver me from this body of death?" (Romans 7:24). Paul answers the question he raised, the abiding question of mankind: "thanks be to God, who gives us the victory through our Lord Jesus Christ" (I Corinthians 15:57).

The good news of the New Testament is precisely that God can do for us what we cannot do for ourselves, and that God has in fact already done it in Christ! God can change our human nature. Conversion is that event in which He changes us, and leads us from the old life dominated by sin into the new life of forgiven fellowship with Him. Conversion is that experience in which we accept Christ's word to us: "You must be born anew."

Conversion becomes possible when a man realizes it is necessary, when a man is reduced to the prayer, "God, be merciful to
me, a sinner." This is a prayer that contemporary activist American Christianity doesn't like to make or hear. A fine church leader
complained to his pastor: "You're always saying that we can't do
anything to achieve salvation by our own efforts. Surely God must
like us more if we obey Him. God helps those who help themselves. It sure can't hurt up there to do a few good deeds down
here."

That man speaks for all of us in our moments of trying to work
our way to heaven. He expresses a particular form of the do-it-
yourself salvation movement which characterizes much of American Protestantism. Of course, good deeds are pleasing to God,
but only when done in gratitude and compassion, never when
done in the hope of piling up a few more points in the heavenly
ledger. Whether we try to save ourselves by good deeds, by aus-
tere disciplines of life, by much religious observance, by much
prophetic social concern—it is the same. Jesus says to us: ". . .
when you have done all that is commanded you, say, 'We are
unworthy servants; we have only done what was our duty'." (Luke
17:10).

This is not to belittle the importance of good works or what
we like to call "Christian character." It is to say that Christian
character is the fruit of Christian discipleship. We can read about
the way in which Christ's character is produced in the fifteenth
chapter of John. The key words are: "I am the vine, you are the
branches. He who abides in me, and I in him, he it is that bears
much fruit, for apart from me you can do nothing" (John 15:5).
Yet the church persists in trying to produce Christian character
in persons who are not disciples of Christ.

A striking illustration of this appears in a statement put out
recently by a Christian institution. Before I quote from it, I
should say that this idea also lies behind much of the religious-
education material that has poured from the presses of liberal
Protestantism in the recent generation.

[This institution] is essentially a religious organization; it is ethi-
cally and spiritually Christian, but it is not dogmatic or ecclesiastical;

it is the purpose of [this institution] not to make Christians but to make persons Christian, that is, to develop Christian character.

Here is a grave misunderstanding of the event in which Christian character is produced. To reiterate, Christian character is the fruit of Christian discipleship. Character follows, never precedes discipleship. So it was that Jesus commanded us to "go and make disciples," not to go and develop Christian character. One is converted to Christ when one becomes a disciple of Christ.

But to go back to Nicodemus. This man was too much of a gentleman to insist on his own righteousness. But he was curious about this business of rebirth. And he wondered in particular, "How can this happen to a man when he's old?" Now we don't know how old Nicodemus was, but if he thought he was old, he must have been old! We may guess that he was more than fifty years of age. He evidently was thinking to himself something like this: "How can I be born anew? My patterns of behavior are set, my relationships have been consummated, my career is well on its way to completion. I'm too old to be changed, to enter into something new."

How many of us have thought the same sort of thing, perhaps at a much earlier age. "I'm married, my career is set, I have dug deep the grooves into which my life will settle. How can I really change very much? How can I swerve the direction of my life?" These are pertinent questions which thinking men will raise, questions which underline the impossibility of becoming changed persons by our own efforts.

You can't do it by yourselves; you won't do it even if you want to badly and try and try and try. With men it is impossible.

But with God, all things are possible—including the rejuvenation, the remaking, the transformation of your life, the deepening of your commitment, the sweetening of your relationships. You, you can be born anew, even when you're old—this is precisely the good news of the New Testament to you. God can change your life!

Elton Trueblood, author and teacher, said in a recent sermon:

There are two insights which can illuminate our understanding of the Christian cause. The first is—the conversion which is important is not conversion from sheer paganism to nominal Christianity, not conversion from cold to warm, but conversion from luke-warm to hot, from a mild religion to one in which a person's whole life is taken up and filled and controlled and compelled. The second insight is that the most common situation in which this kind of conversion can occur is the situation of middle age.

If we increase the span of middle age somewhat more than is comfortable for many of us to include, roughly the years from thirty to sixty, it is clear that it is within this age range that large numbers of persons are converted genuinely and permanently to Christ. The gentle, imperceptible work of the Holy Spirit may have been working in a man's soul for years, from his youth on, but again and again the explosion of new life comes in the middle years: when a man has lived long enough to learn something of the intractability of life, of his own gross limitations, of the mortality of all things; when life has hurt him or struck him down or just bored him; when he has discovered that he isn't going to be president of the company, ever; or, when having become president of the company, he has discovered there is still the vague but yawning emptiness within himself at the core of his being. Then he begins to understand his need of something or someone. Then he becomes vulnerable as never before; his pleasures leave him unsatisfied; his work leaves him unfulfilled; and he begins looking and searching. How can a man be born again when he is old? Why that's precisely when it happens!

But Nicodemus wasn't yet satisfied. He was in this sense a modern, a man we can understand; for he wanted to know *how* this rebirth takes place, the mechanics of the thing. He wanted a blueprint, a time schedule of conversion. And Jesus replied to his question: "The wind blows where it wills, and you hear the sound of it, but you do not know whence it comes or whither it goes; so it is with every one who is born of the Spirit" (John 3:8).

There is mystery in the working of God; there is surprise and unexpectedness in the power of the Holy Spirit. We can see sometimes the fruit, the real evidence of converted and changing lives before our eyes, but we can't rationalize it all, we can't figure it all out, because we can't figure God out. There is a holiness, an awe about conversion; there is a sense in which we must not probe into grace. It is precisely my own experience of the working of the Holy Spirit that He comes in ways we don't expect, and in circumstances which appear least propitious. He has His own time schedule, and we do not know it. This is part of the tremendous joy and amazement which are ours when He moves into our lives, bearing witness with our spirits, awakening us to new life.

This is the amazing fact of our time. Lives are being changed. The Holy Spirit is at work in the world reaching into the midst of dull, drab, routinized living, or into the darkness of some tragedy, to awaken, arouse, uproot, and replant persons. The evidence of His power and presence in changed and changing lives announces the coming of the Spirit to this generation, as on the day of Pentecost when the church was born. New creation is appearing in the church. Persons are being converted.

In the next few chapters of this book we shall be exploring the nature of this conversion experience, in order to discover how we may be used of the Spirit to help usher people into this event of transformation. We can learn how to prepare ourselves and others to receive the Spirit.

But before we leave Nicodemus, we may speculate that perhaps he asked Jesus one more question, though if so it was never recorded. For the question which naturally arises out of such an encounter with Jesus is: "What then can I do? Indeed, is there anything I can do, except wait around for the Spirit to come?" Jesus told Nicodemus that the Holy Spirit comes unannounced and unsummoned, like the wind. We know something about when and where the wind blows; and if we want to stand in the wind, we can go where we have observed it blowing in times past, and wait and pray. We have learned, we of Christ's church, some things about when and where the Holy Spirit does His transforming, converting work. If we want to be transformed, converted, we can go into the places and situations where the Spirit has been working in our generation, and wait and pray expectantly. Bernard A. Weisberger has written a fascinating account of the great revivalists and their influence on American religious life. He describes the crowds of people that came to the old-time camp meetings:

A mixture of motives brought the Kentuckians from far and near to the log church at Gaspar River. They were looking for a rare chance to hobnob with neighbors unseen for a year at a stretch. They hoped for entertainment in the form of rousing sermons, and a chance to let out feelings which were cramped up by a hog and hominy existence. But it is important to remember that fundamentally they were expecting to be converted by divine influence. Put simply, they came expecting a miracle.[3]

Strategies change, and many people today wouldn't seek the Holy Spirit in a camp meeting, though let us not be so narrow that we call such meetings out-of-bounds for the Holy Spirit. There are specific situations today where the Holy Spirit has been coming in power, and these we shall be considering. But the important thing, for us as for those country folk of a hundred years ago, is that we come to our churches, our prayers, our daily work, the reading of the Bible, *expecting to be converted by divine influence. Put simply, we come expecting a miracle.*

Remember Jesus' words: ". . . how much more will the heavenly Father give the Holy Spirit to those who ask him?" (Luke 11:13).

III

Conversion Begins in Awakening

Awake, O sleeper, and arise from the dead, and
Christ shall give you light.

EPHESIANS 5:14

The film *The Horse's Mouth* tells the story of a Bohemian
painter who lives on a houseboat. There is one scene where a
young admirer of the artist asks him why and how he became a
painter. The man looks out through the broken window as though
at something far away and says: "One time I saw a painting by
the artist Matisse. I was stunned and suddenly saw the world in
color, as though for the first time. He skinned my eyes; I became
a different man; it was like a conversion."

He skinned my eyes; I became a different man; it was like a
conversion; he lifted the veil from my seeing; I saw things differently, in color and dimension and meaning. Haven't you had
some such moment of revelation when suddenly something quite
common and ordinary seemed filled with glory and beauty as
never before? A parent may have such a moment of grace bending
over his child in the darkened room as the child sleeps with the
light on her tender, innocent face; and suddenly he knows that
he is in the presence of the mystery and wonder of a soul God
has created. A young man may enter into such an experience
when suddenly, looking upon a girl, he discovers that he is in
love with her and wants to marry her. A scientist or a schoolboy
may have such a revelation in looking through the microscope
upon the miracle of life, or through the telescope into the mystery and movement of outer space.

Edmund Fuller describes an experience of awakening that

31

comes to a writer when "the idea" strikes him: "He sees himself as one who through the mystery of grace has had his eyes opened to perceive that which it has not been given to his contemporaries to see. He longs to share with them the insight and the vision which, he knows not why or how, has been given him."[1]

Conversion begins when the Holy Spirit enlightens the eyes of our hearts in some moment of awakening. We suddenly find ourselves looking about to discover "Who am I? Where am I going? What is the meaning of my life?" When we awaken in the new day, we are hungry and thirsty. So now, "My soul is hungry and thirsty; there is an emptiness within me which cries out for fulfillment, something or someone missing at the core of my being." We begin to wonder and wander in search of it or him. We ask, we seek, we knock. This is the beginning of conversion.

It is often a disturbing time, for we are no longer content with things as they are, or with ourselves as we are. We feel a lack; we are restless, discontent, and perhaps aware of a rising expectancy. We grope, trying to break out of the spiritual shell in which we are imprisoned until light comes into the dark cave of our hibernation, and with it a voice saying: "Awake, O sleeper, and arise from the dead, and Christ shall give you light." We are apprehended by God in some event in which, potentially, life may never again be the same.

There are varieties of awakening. No one pattern or blueprint fits all of us; God moves in mysterious ways in our hearts, and we can never specifically anticipate His coming. But we can say that God wakens some of us rudely, and others more gently. We talk about a rude awakening, as though one were roughly thrown out of bed onto the floor and shaken into wakefulness.

The Late Liz is a fascinating autobiography of a woman of our day who was rudely awakened by the Holy Spirit. She was living in the top level of American society, "the real upper class," according to Vance Packard's analysis in *The Status Seekers*. She suffered through three broken marriages. Finally she became so riddled with hurt and bitterness that one night she took thirteen high-dosage sleeping pills in an attempt to commit suicide. Her son found her unconscious on her bed some time later. She was rushed to the hospital, where she hung between life and death for hours, and then slowly awakened—an awakening which was to

be a total personal awakening, in soul as well as body. Her remembrance of these moments of awakening is, in part, this:

> The one implicit feeling was a sense of freedom, of being in all
> ways unencumbered, as though my windows had been washed, as
> though some part of me were left behind, a part old and hard and
> heavy. . . . My mind was sharply clear; it too was washed and un-
> encumbered, and it was waiting, and the sense of expectancy was
> very strong. . . .

Her eyes focused on a glass container, whereupon she realized
that she was in a hospital.

> The world in which I lay was a very private world and I was quite
> alone. And then, all at once, I was not alone. There was no increase
> in light, no sound, no motion, no scent. Lying utterly still I waited.
> Unable to accept, I was now accepting, letting myself be claimed,
> letting this something mount and permeate and cover the self I'd
> been, as the tide rises to cover what was formerly dry and bare. And
> now I knew what this was, this was the Father, here was the Glory
> of the patient presence. Wonder came, and with the wonder, peace
> —not the peace the world knows but an in-going, at-oneness; and I
> understood, I understood that I had been forgiven.[2]

This woman is the mother of one of my dearest friends. I
know her personally. And I know that God has literally awakened
her to a new life in which she has grown in grace and power to
become one of the most effective witnesses for Christ of our time.
She has told her story to many groups: college people, church
congregation of many denominations and races, groups of Alcoholics Anonymous, businessmen's groups, women's groups.

Some people are thus rudely awakened by God. If you have
been in some crisis or some tragedy or some awful falling through
the open trap door, you will recognize parts of your own experience in the awakening of Elizabeth Burns. One who is tormented
by the agonies of alcoholism and who finally hits bottom may
know what this means. If that person is lucky, he will wake up
in the alcoholic ward of a hospital and look into the face of a
member of Alcoholics Anonymous.

The Prodigal Son in Jesus' parable was rudely awakened. The
terse biblical verse puts it this way: "he came to himself"—and

that's always the way it is; one comes to oneself, faces oneself and the world honestly and cleanly in the presence of God.

Sometimes one is rudely awakened to God by a personal defeat of some sort, a drastic illness, a crushing failure in business, or some period of suffering in which he discovers his own weakness, the sand of his own vanishing powers. He cries out for help and receives the touch of healing grace, the renewing of strength which comes from without to sustain him.

One man who had such an experience was an aggressive, hard-sell salesman, and a good one. He was an utterly self-confident man, with no apparent weaknesses. Several years ago he had a mental breakdown, had to spend two weeks in the hospital, and went through a period of several months under psychiatric help before he grew back to mental and spiritual health. In the midst of what was a terrible personal experience, this man cried out for God, and he is convinced that God helped him come out of his trouble. He came into a Bible Study Group and began to grow into Christian maturity. He has become a leader in the church; he has become one of the most truly compassionate persons I know. Last Christmas a letter came from him, part of which reads as follows:

This Christmas means a lot to me for many reasons, one of which is that I feel that not only do I have a closer understanding of God and God's work, but that I am a changing person spiritually. I had been riding fast and hard and high for so many years. Then when a tumble threw me several years ago, it was then that I experienced a quick and sudden realization of what life is all about. How small and insignificant I really was, and how much I had still to learn about really helping other people.

It is horrible to be in left field alone and trying all by yourself to reach and grasp for a shred of straw. And then, all of a sudden, how wonderful to experience the strength of God and to realize that I had a multitude of friends, not against me, but with me.

That man was blasted awake in an experience which was the beginning of his conversion.

Now for every one thus rudely awakened, there must be hundreds who are gently awakened by God. Whittaker Chambers describes such a gentle awakening:

I was sitting in our apartment on St. Paul Street in Baltimore. . . .

My daughter was in her high chair. I was watching her eat. She was the most miraculous thing that had ever happened in my life. I liked to watch her even when she smeared porridge on her face or dropped it meditatively on the floor. My eye came to rest on the delicate convolutions of her ear—those intricate, perfect ears. The thought passed through my mind: "No, those ears were not created by any chance coming together of atoms in nature (the Communist view). They could have been created only by immense design." The thought was involuntary and unwanted. I crowded it out of my mind. But I never wholly forgot it or the occasion. . . . I did not then know that, at that moment, the finger of God was first laid upon my forehead.[3]

Those who have grown up in Christian homes, whose parents have shared real Christian marriage, who have been nurtured in the fellowship of the church from the beginning, have been gently awakened. Their eyes of faith have opened like those of a newly born baby, slowly, gradually, until finally they came to see the glory of light. Their conversion began imperceptibly, unsensationally, quietly. And one day they learned to sing in remembrance, "Breathe on me, breath of God, fill me with life anew," for in months and years of such "breathing," they were being awakened by God.

And for some, this gentle awakening of God is followed by faithful response, and the person just seems to grow in grace from very childhood, to pledge mature commitment when the time comes, never to suffer doubt or uncertainty, partaking all the while of eternal life. Such persons are truly blessed of God. They are rare exceptions within the life of the church.

Most of us who have been gently awakened in the Christian nursery of our homes and nurtured within the church come to a period in our lives when we stop growing. This happens to us when we begin to lose interest and fall by the wayside. We may encounter real doubt or go to sleep again inwardly, while outwardly we are conquering new worlds of schooling and work, piling up reputation, and achieving our little successes. We may have kept up the forms of church membership and even of involvement in the church's activity, but we have lost the power of the Spirit. Quietly and unconsciously the soul is withering away.

So, many of us within the life of the organized church slumber along spiritually, without power from on high, without grace, in a barren and fruitless and strangely disquieting existence until— one day we are awakened again. It may be in a moment of prayer when God suddenly breaks through the curtain of our indifference and rouses us to confession. It may be in a service of worship when an old hymn strikes a chord of memory long forgotten, now remembered with a rush of meaning. We find ourselves with lumps in our throats, winking back the tears. It may be in a fellowship where we are studying the Bible and sharing personal experience with others, when in a moment we *know* we do trust God, wholly and utterly. It may be on a retreat where, in quietness, we discover ourselves in new dimension, and return home to become new persons for God. It may be a chance word in a sermon, a friendship formed, one of an infinite variety of ways in which the Holy Spirit touches the heart, and we shake out the cobwebs, and the eye of faith begins to see again. God skins our eyes.

It is a main task of the church to provide the conditions and circumstances in which God may awaken people, or reawaken them. Church leaders must learn how to prepare people for conversion. We must lead our people into those places where the wind blows, where the Holy Spirit is working. It is this writer's conviction that the most propitious conditions for awakening prevail in *koinonia* groups centering on Bible study. These groups will be described in detail in later chapters of this book. For the moment, consider the experience of a woman awakened in this context. She and her husband had been in a Bible Study Group for many months. On the evening when it was their responsibility to lead in the opening devotions, she asked if she might share an experience which had recently been hers. Here is part of what she read to us:

In a state of restlessness and confusion, my mind searched endlessly to evolve a philosophy that would give me the security of self-identification. My intellect refused to give me a satisfying answer.

Because my church was alert to my need, I was led to find the answer. I found myself in a Bible Study Group where I was stimulated to read and study the Bible and re-think the Christian faith of which I had been a life-long member. This led me further into more feverish searching where I read furiously, talked endlessly, where the urgency of the search crowded everything else from my thoughts.

One morning while working at a very routine household chore, my mind surged ahead relentlessly, like a tide engulfing me, revealing with great clarity the meaning of Christ's life, death, and resurrection. It was a moment of illumination. I accepted this quickening as the true reality behind my senses. Purpose and meaning to life followed. I found hope, not despair, a Way of Life, not a philosophy. I caught a glimpse of a greater purpose, a larger perspective. I was a small part of that omnipotent plan. In finding God, I also found myself. I needed no further identification. I prayed thankfully.

In the days that followed, I felt as if I had just emerged from a fog and I expected to see a dramatic change, a sharp contrast from black to white. I was disappointed. And yet, was there a more subtle change? Now I was aware of my obligation to serve God and my fellow man. I was keenly aware of the importance of all the mundane obscure events of my days, and the countless small omissions. It was significant to me that I had been actively working when I had this experience.

That woman and her husband began to teach the high-school class in their church. They began to fulfill their "obligation to serve God and my fellow man." Some time ago she wrote: "Our spiritual awakening is still so fresh and new that we still marvel and can scarcely believe the changes in our lives."

There ought to be scores of people in every local church being thus awakened by God, coming into the vestibule of conversion.

When the time is ripe in God's fullness, the Holy Spirit breathes upon a man. The miracle of conversion begins, as strangely and wondrously as when a doctor takes a newly born baby not yet breathing, and, placing his own mouth over the mouth of that already dying child, literally breathes new life into him, filling those infant lungs with his own breath and drawing forth the response that will mean life.

Precious is the moment of awakening; it is a strange meeting place of apathy and excitement, of time and eternity, of death and life. In Michelangelo's fresco "The Creation," Adam reclines, leaning on an elbow with hand hanging loose, fingers limp in life-lessness. In sharp contrast, God, dynamic with power, stretches His arm straight toward Adam, His forefinger alive with creative spark, about to touch Adam's dead finger—in the holy moment of conversion, resurrection, new creation.

IV

Conversion Continues by Decision

And Jesus said to them, "Follow me. . . ." And immediately they left their nets and followed him.

MARK 1:17, 18

William Larimer Mellon, Jr., retired at the age of thirty-seven with everything one could want: family, money, prestige, and a life of leisure and pleasure ahead of him. One night he read a magazine article which was to change his life. It was about Dr. Albert Schweitzer who, years before, at the age of thirty, had put aside successful careers in music, writing, and teaching to go to Africa as a medical missionary.

An idea began to grow in Mellon's mind. He read all he could find about Dr. Schweitzer, eventually corresponding with him. Then the day came when Mellon made his decision. He recalls: "I found Gwen [his wife] on a ladder doing housework. I went to her and blurted out, 'I think I'll go to medical school, then settle down somewhere that can use a good country doctor.'"

The rest is simply told. He went to Tulane University. Upon graduation, he decided to work in the disease-ridden tropics of Haiti. Today he is the chief doctor of the first hospital in that area, a hospital which was built with his money. Mellon's life has been utterly changed, converted. And it happened because he had the courage to make a decision.

Thousands of other people read the same magazine article and put it aside, thanking God for such a man as Dr. Schweitzer and perhaps even praying that God would raise up other such men to serve Him. But for Mellon, this article was an awakening, a soul-opening, a lifting of the veil, a skinning of the eyes of faith.

God did His part; He awakened Larry Mellon. And then it was up to Mellon. The conversion of his life depended on one thing: his own decision to accept the tugging in his soul, to say "yes" to the rising hope in him, and to give his life to an unknown venture in faith.

If conversion begins in *awakening*, it continues only by *decision*. The Holy Spirit touches us, jars us, in whatever way awakens us, so that there is suddenly before us an infinite horizon of possibility. Then we decide. We say "yes," or "no," or "I don't know," and the great opportunity has been dealt with according to our decision. God takes the initiative with us, but if any permanent turning of life is to take place, each man must make his own personal affirmation to God. Each must face himself and God in his own awakening, expose himself in honesty to the meaning of the encounter, and say "yes" to the leading. Only by personal decision does conversion continue, as the conversion of Larry Mellon hung on his decision.

A number of years ago I stood on the northwestern shores of the Sea of Galilee. For centuries the fishermen waded out into the shallow, warm water to cast their nets for fish. I stood and watched a man casting his net, flinging it out in the manner of a backhand tennis stroke, the net flying out over the water, settling in, and then slowly drawn back with its hoped-for catch. This was the very area where history's most famous fishermen—Peter, Andrew, James, John—were doing their work when Jesus stopped by their boats and called to them. The Gospel according to Mark, in characteristic fashion, pictures this turning point in the history of the world in terse, tension-filled words: "Jesus said to them, 'Follow me and I will make you become fishers of men.' And immediately they left their nets and followed him."

Just like that. They left their nets and followed Him. We are left to speculate on the details of this encounter. We don't know whether these men had previously met or known Jesus; we don't know what further conversation there was. All we know is this: these men saw and heard Jesus; He gave them an invitation, a command, and they said "yes" to Him. They could have shrugged their shoulders and continued mending the nets and fishing, as countless others then and since have shrugged off personal encounters with Christ. They found themselves face to face with

Christ in a moment of decision; they made a decision for Christ.

A decision for Christ. Why is that phrase embarrassing to us? When we hear it we get uneasy and almost look around, fearing lest someone take us by the shoulder and ask us if we have been saved. This phrase makes us uneasy and even afraid, for very good reason. For it implies a very personal, particular commitment to a Person, Jesus Christ, in which one becomes totally involved, takes a specific stand, and finds himself exposed and risked. We are afraid of being involved and committed; we don't want to risk anything, especially ourselves. We don't want to lose our lives. Who in his right mind would want to take up a cross?

And besides, it isn't smart these days to be enthusiastic about anyone more important than the latest home-run hitter or Brigitte Bardot. We smile faintly and with condescension at political and religious "fanatics." Ours is the spirit of *comme ci, comme ça.* The noncommitment typical of our time is well symbolized by the chapel, or meditation room in the United Nations' General Assembly building in New York. The symbols of all religions have been banished lest any of the world's religions be offended. The room is empty except for some chairs and, in the center, a polished tree trunk on top of which is a cluster of philodendron, illuminated by a shaft of light. Marya Mannes describes the spiritual impact of this room:

> It seemed to me standing there that this nothingness was so oppressive and disturbing that it became a sort of madness, and the room a sort of padded cell. It seemed to me that the core of our greatest contemporary trouble lay here, that all this whiteness and shapelessness and weakness was the leukemia of non-commitment sapping our strength. We had found, finally, that only nothing could please all. . . .[1]

And so it is perfectly natural that we should rationalize our weakness and impotence by putting a brand on the words "decision for Christ." We relegate the words and the experience to the sawdust trail or the aisle of an arena crusade, while thinking to ourselves: "This business of 'decision for Christ' is for people who like their religion hot and heavy, chiefly those who generally get overly excited about it all; but not for me; not for reasonable, dignified, well-bred me; I like my religion quiet and always in good taste."

We forget that the New Testament is not good taste but good news! And if news is really good—like the end of a long war, or the discovery of a man thought dead, or the healing of a loved one feared dying, or the coming of Almighty God to earth in person—then this news is worth getting excited about; it's worth all we are and have!

But in our time, millions favor what has been called "religion in general," the sort of religion in vogue in Hollywood's "religious" movies, the sort that is selling well on the newsstands. A perfect example of it is the compilation of credos in Edward R. Murrow's book *This I Believe*. A cursory look through that book reveals the fact that there is a good deal of "I," much use of the word "believe," but very little "this." The average contributor lines up in favor of God, motherhood, native land, and free enterprise, but beyond that he is vague and uncommitted. So we indulge in the superficiality of easy, costless tolerance, indifferent to what others believe, because we neither know nor seem to care what we believe. This is religion-at-a-distance, a comfortable distance; and it should surprise no one that such religion produces no real change in a man's life.

For Christianity is not primarily a creed, though we must spell out in systematic fashion what we do believe; nor is Christianity primarily a code of ethics, though we must clarify and pursue the social implications of our faith. Christianity at heart is a *total personal commitment to Jesus Christ*. It is nothing other than, or less than, a personal relationship with Him. This relationship requires conscious decision on our part.

Several years ago I spent a few days on the campus of Yale University, assisting in a Billy Graham mission to the University. It was a fascinating, eye-opening experience. I learned something valuable during those days, and I learned it from Billy Graham. I learned that when the New Testament message is presented squarely and directly, without apology, with deep conviction, people respond. Some say "yes," some say "no," but few remain indifferent. People are summoned to personal decision. I watched many young men make specific decisions to do something, or to stop doing something, or to try something. Doubtless many such decisions had little permanent effect, for if conversion is to be permanent, decision must lead into growth and be sustained by discipline. But I am still in correspondence with one young man whose life today is different because of the four days of the Billy Graham mission. And there are others.

The point is, I learned not to look down my nose automatically at decisions made in crusades and rallies because I discovered that some of those decisions would result, in time, in permanently changed lives. You may remember when Billy Graham was going to New York for a crusade there, Protestant clergymen came out both for and against him. Reinhold Niebuhr, a top-flight theologian, took what appeared to be a thoroughly negative view of Graham's coming, "as though the eye were to say to the hand, I have no need of you."

Henry Pitney Van Dusen, the president of Union Theological Seminary where Dr. Niebuhr has been a world-famous teacher, said this:

> There are many, of whom I am one, who are not ashamed to testify that they would probably never have come within the sound of Dr. Niebuhr's voice or the influence of his mind if they had not first been touched by the message of the earlier Billy [Billy Sunday]. Quite probably five or ten years hence there may appear in the classrooms and churches of Billy Graham's severest critics not a few who will be glad to give parallel testimony to his role in starting them in that direction.[3]

And that's the whole point. We start in the direction of Christian discipleship when we decide to say "yes" to Christ. One does not become a Christian overnight, but he may make the first step overnight or in a moment of decision. In the next chapter we shall consider how one grows in faith, how one grows toward maturity in Christ. But there can be no growth unless and until there is decision; one can make no progress along the road until one decides to take the road. As someone has written: "So many in our churches are busily continuing something they never anywhere decisively began." One does not become a Christian by receiving secondhand the faith of his fathers; no one becomes a Christian *in absentia*, or by default, or in his sleep; one *decides* to follow Christ.

If there is to be marriage between a man and woman who have been going together, there must come the moment when they decide to be married. That moment may appear to be or even truly be spontaneous. More often the moment comes after some period of acquaintance. But the moment must come if there is to be a permanent relationship of commitment. Many good church members have been "going around" with Christ for years without ever having made an adult commitment of life to Him, without having become involved with Christ, without having entered into firsthand fellowship with Him.

What would a decision for Christ mean for you? It could mean an abrupt, radical change of life—if you are the Prodigal Son type. If you were to diagram his "decision," it would be drawn as a line going in one direction, and then a sudden turnabout, going in the opposite direction. When the Prodigal Son "came to himself," he decided to reject the life in which he was then engaged and to return to his father. His decision to go back home was founded on repentance. Jesus put priority on the necessity of repentance in the sum of His gospel as Mark relates it: "Repent, and believe in the gospel" (Mark 1:15).

To repent means to have a change of mind, heart, and will. It means to take a new direction of life. It means to give up the old life and enter upon the new life. An alcoholic who comes to himself in the fellowship of Alcoholics Anonymous makes such an abrupt change of direction. He repents by rejecting totally the practice which enslaved him. He turns from the old life and takes up the new. Anyone who is living in dishonesty or infidelity of any sort must make such an abrupt turnabout if he is to decide for Christ. A man who in schizophrenic fashion thinks he can accept the new life without letting go of the old, without giving up the fruits of past sinful behavior, will discover it can't be done. Shakespeare provides a telling illustration of this in Hamlet. Claudius has murdered his brother and now reigns in his brother's place as king. He feels guilty, and would pray.

> O! my offence is rank, it smells to heaven;
>
> . . . .
> . . . . Pray can I not,
> Though inclination be as sharp as will:
> My stronger guilt defeats my strong intent;
> And, like a man to double business bound,
> I stand in pause where I shall first begin,
> And both neglect. . . .

> . . . .
> My fault is past. But, O! what form of prayer
> Can serve my turn? "Forgive me my foul murder"?
> That cannot be; since I am still possess'd
> Of those effects for which I did the murder,
> My crown, mine own ambition, and my queen.
> May one be pardon'd and retain the offence?
>
> . . . .
> Try what repentance can: what can it not?
> Yet what can it, when one can not repent?"

Claudius continues his efforts at prayer and finally gives up, saying:

> My words fly up, my thoughts remain below:
> Words without thoughts never to heaven go.[2]

Honest repentance must underlie any genuine turning to God. One may not "be pardon'd and retain the offence." When Zacchaeus "decided for Christ" (Luke 19:1–10), his decision to repay old debts and extortions was that repentance which is always the other side of the coin of commitment. If a man is in Christ, the old must pass away in order that the new may come. For some people, decision for Christ will mean a radical change of direction.

Many other people would have a more gradual curve of decision for Christ, something like the wake of a boat as the boat slowly curves around to go in the opposite direction. If you have been living a happy pagan existence, apart from the church or on the fringes of the church, busily engaged in climbing the ladder of success, this could be your experience. For one day comes the winter of discontent. Life is a bit stale; the hopes and promises have not been fulfilled. You cast a look over your shoulder at Christ and His people and wonder, and maybe you wander into church some Sunday morning. You find yourself alerted and questioning, and before long participating, and all at once involved and challenged to commit yourself to Christ. As you look back, you see that you were making many little decisions, slowly turning about until suddenly you were face to face with Christ, walking in fellowship with Him. The big decision was made in parts, and almost though never really imperceptibly.

But most of those persons who have grown up within the church have been zigzagging along in the general direction of Christ. Early in life they were positioned toward Christ, and they have been meandering His way more or less ever since. If asked, "Are you Christian?" they would say, "Of course. All respectable people are." If asked, "Have you decided for Christ?," they would grow uneasy and look around for the door.

And then something happens—that marvelous, fresh time of awakening to decision, when you stop meandering, and make choices. This happened to the writer as a junior at Yale, in a philosophy class. My teacher, a Jew, a magnificent person and teacher, forced me to consider what I did think of this man Jesus. Was He a good man, was He a deluded man, was He the best man, was He Savior and Lord? What did those words mean? I realized under the pressure of this confrontation that I had made no real decisions in these matters. At that point I stopped zigzagging and began to ask, seek, and knock.

I have watched scores of people in the life of a local church stop like that, and begin asking, seeking, and knocking—people who have received, have found, have had the door of grace opened to them.

It is the job of leaders in the church to help people make meaningful decisions for Christ. We must come close to people and stay close to them, watching for the time and circumstance of significant decision. This means a willingness to be patient, to wait on the Lord, to respect the Holy Spirit. It means that we cannot pressure people into specific decisions which happen to conform to our time schedule of convenience. It means that we are sensitive to the moments of revelation, of new discovery that come to people, always hoping that these moments may become "awakenings." We are to guide people who are awakened into the making of meaningful decisions. For one man, a first decision may be the determination to worship regularly every Sunday. For another person, conversion may continue by the decision to take prayer seriously, to pray every day, with specific guides. For yet another, it may be necessary to decide to do some reading in the area of major doubts and uncertainties. Or, a decisive change may come with the willingness to make a sacrificial financial pledge. It is the writer's conviction that the most permanently hopeful decision an "awakened person" could be helped to make would be a decision to come into a *koinonia group* (see Chapter VII). In such a group the conditions for continuing conversion are the best. When one becomes involved in a *koinonia* group, his "decision" is not hidden in individual intention, easily reached and more easily neglected. It is corporate, public, shared. In such a group he finds the mutual encouragement necessary for the continuance of conversion.

If church leaders are to perform this crucial ministry to the "awakened," they must be prepared to direct much attention and time and energy to it. There is implied here a major revision of the role of the clergy, the nature and purpose of the special ministry to which the clergy is called. We shall return to this matter in Chapter XII. For the moment our concern is to help people "decide for Christ" in whatever ways are presently meaningful to them.

Several years ago Bishop Stephen Neill conducted a Yale University Mission. At the end of one of his talks he summoned each person present to take a pencil and piece of paper when back in his room, and write: "I commit as much as I know of myself to as much as I know of God in Christ." Conversion continues by such decision.

V

Conversion Matures by Growth

> . . . we are meant . . . to grow up in every way
> into Christ. . . . until . . . we arrive at real ma-
> turity—that measure of development which is meant
> by "the fullness of Christ."
>
> EPHESIANS 4:15, 13, Phillips

The automatic pilot in modern airplanes is a fascinating device. Once the airplane is aloft and directed toward its destination, the automatic pilot is put into action, the controls set, and the human pilot can sit back and relax while the airplane continues perfectly on its course, guaranteed to keep on the beam.

Many church people have what may be called an "automatic-pilot" concept of the Christian life. We think that once our sights are lifted, and we are aloft and directed toward Christ, on the Christian way, then we can set the controls to automatic pilot and float into the heavenly city. Being members of the church just about guarantees that we will stay on the beam (so we suppose); we can sit back and relax, taking it easy, assuming that we will be carried safely to our destination.

There's only one flaw in the automatic-pilot theory of the Christian life—it doesn't work! The reason is, there is nothing automatic about the Christian life. One decides for or against Christ every day of his life in all his decision-making. It is a crucial decision to have turned one's life toward Christ and committed oneself to Him; but that is when the real struggle begins. Conversion has a beginning in our awakening to decision, but if conversion is to be permanent, it has no ending, for we are called now to walk the way we have chosen. The author of Ephesians wrote to the Christian people at Ephesus: "We are not meant

47

to remain as children at the mercy of every chance wind of teaching. . . . But we are meant to hold firmly to the truth in love, and to grow up in every way into Christ, the head. . . . until . . . we arrive at real maturity—that measure of development which is meant by 'the fullness of Christ' " (Ephesians 4:14, 15, 13, Phillips).

Conversion is not only an initial act; it is a growing experience! For no one of us is ever fully, totally converted to Christ. There are pockets of resistance; there is falling *from* grace as well as growing *in* grace. There are denials and betrayals as well as courageous affirmations. No matter how old we may be, or how intelligent, or how ordinary, or how extraordinary, we all begin at the beginning as baby Christians. Paul wrote to the Christians in Corinth: "But I, brethren, could not address you as spiritual men, . . . but as babes in Christ. I fed you with milk, not solid food; for you were not ready for it; and even yet you are not ready . . ." (I Corinthians 3:1, 2).

It takes time to become a Christian. One is not genuinely converted to Christ overnight. Paul was writing out of his own experience, for it was a full three years after his awakening on the Damascus road when he entered upon his active ministry. The three years probably were spent in a monastic setting near Damascus, where Paul sought to understand the meaning of what had happened to him and the mission to which he was now called. For us, too, it will take time. Harry Emerson Fosdick wrote: "Such transformation of life does not happen in a moment; it requires more than instantaneous exposure to take the Lord's picture on a human heart; but the time-exposure will do it. . . ."

We must qualify Fosdick's statement by saying that the "exposure" must be in the particular environment of *koinonia*, and the "time" is in fact a lifetime. The church must prepare her people for a lifetime of growth. With one hand the church reaches out to awaken persons to decision for Christ; with the other hand the church guides persons to grow up in every way into Christ. The church is both evangelist and educator, both obstetrician and pediatrician, helping deliver those newly born in Christ and nurturing them from infancy to maturity in Christ. The pastor corrects the evangelist by preparing his people for the struggle of growth.

What then shall we look for as we "grow up into Christ"? What is the nature of this struggle? What are we to expect along this way? We are to expect growing pains. What we may have thought to be a crown now is discovered to look more and more like a cross. Olive Wyon, in her book *On the Way*, describes this matter of moving from the honeymoon stage of Christian life into the "for better, for worse" state of commitment to Christ:

The initial stages of conversion—especially if this has taken a sudden or striking form—are usually very happy. The released soul is conscious of a great sense of freedom, and is eager to speak of this to others, to try to win others to Christ. All this is very natural, and it is indeed the work of God. But, as time goes on, very often the first bright light grows dim; there is no longer a heightened sense of emotional response to God. Prayer, which has hitherto been easy and delightful, has now become dry and dull. Even the Bible seems insipid. Worst of all—and this is very bewildering—sins which we had thought we had left behind forever, begin to rear their ugly heads again, and torment us more than ever. If we can bring ourselves to speak about this we say: "Instead of being better, I find that I am worse."[1]

We all go through these times of depression and dryness in our spiritual life when the honeymoon is over, the romantic glow of our early turning to God is fading, and we have to face the realistic business of making this commitment work and grow toward maturity. We are now entering the severest struggle of life, the struggle to overcome ourselves.

Some time ago a young couple in their mid-thirties began to take Christian life quite seriously. They joined a Bible Study Group and worked hard at forging Christian faith. After they had been in the Study Group some months, one of them wrote to me, saying this:

After our last Bible Study Group, we got to talking about church membership and Christian discipleship. We quickly agreed that the terms were not synonymous, and we were wondering when, if ever, the one turned into the other. When we first joined this group we were assured that it was the turning of our steps in the direction of Christ, as the Galilean fisherman had done, that counted—that it was the committing as much as we knew of ourselves to as much as we knew about God that mattered. But now that we know more about God and more about ourselves, the decision is becoming a lot more difficult. We realize rather sharply that we aren't Christians, and we aren't making much progress. Where have we gone wrong? Is this a common experience?

Yes, it's a common experience all right, but a very uncommon understanding of the continuing travail of deciding for Christ against oneself. This is the never-ending battle of "not my will, but thine be done." By nature we want to save our lives, not lose them. By nature we want to do our will, no one else's. By nature we do not want to take up the cross. Even as we grow in Christ we find ourselves overwhelmed and humbled by our tyrannical self-will. Paul wrote out of such agonizing struggle in his attempt to do God's will: "I do not understand my own actions. For I do not do what I want, but I do the very thing I hate. . . . I can will what is right, but I cannot do it. For I do not do the good I want, but the evil I do not want is what I do. . . . Wretched man that I am! Who will deliver me from this body of death?" (Romans 7:15, 18, 19, 24).

The deep and searing pains of growth remind us that we are sinners. Our continuing growth comes only out of continuing repentance and ever-new decision for Christ. We are always engaged in the struggle to deny ourselves and affirm God. We are forever dependent on God for the power to do His will. We need help—the rootage of disciplined commitment, the encouragement of sustaining fellowship. We are not sufficient unto ourselves.

The question raised by the young couple in the Study Group represents deep and permanent growth into Christ. For the amazing paradox is precisely that we are growing most when we think we are growing least. And we are growing least when we think we are growing most, in the times when we are satisfied with our spiritual progress. St. John of the Cross writes: "The soul makes greatest progress when it least thinks so, yes most frequently when it thinks it is losing ground. The soul makes greatest progress when it travels in the dark, not knowing the way."[2]

We must not be upset or thrown off course by our falls from grace. We must expect them and be ready for the times when we just don't want to pray, when we're ready to give up, when we're afflicted with the most common virus sweeping through entire congregations: don't care-ism. There isn't a man alive who is free from temptations or gnawing doubts. When these come, or when a psycho-physical fatigue settles upon us, we know that God can use these times to test us, to deepen our capacity to trust Him, forcing us to rely totally on Him, to walk in faith because we cannot see the way ahead.

I have learned through personal experience that God gives growth in time of adversity. When I first came to the church I presently serve, several years ago, there had been some difficulty in that church. Things were not well, and morale was poor and slipping. In the self-confidence of youth, I supposed that a few weeks under my leadership would serve to get us on the way upward and onward. After more than three months of constant prayer and the hardest work I knew how to produce, the situation in the church was showing no signs of recovery. For the first time in my life I was facing a situation in which I was being forced to admit my inadequacy. I was doing all I could, yet seemingly to no avail. I began to question not only my capacity under God to turn the tide in this church but also my own vocation as a minister. As the weeks wore on with little to encourage me, I was literally forced to my knees, the pride being crushed out of me, until I could only pray, "God, I cannot do this. If You want it done, You must do it."

During this lowest period in my life, my wife and I spent a few days with my parents, talking it all over, praying about it, and finding new strength in their fellowship. We returned to face the same situation, but we ourselves were not the same. It was the early part of October. Over a period of several days, when still there were no overt signs of encouragement, I began to entrust myself and the whole enterprise to God. Before the recovery was manifest, I was enabled to accept whatever might be God's will. A deep inner peace became the foundation whereon I could stand, and I found that I could trust God without external evidence. "Grace in October" was the most real knowledge of God's power and love which had yet been mine. God gave to me the gracious gift of trust. God gave to us all the power for new life. I discovered that the grace of God is His saving help to him who is helpless.

When you feel beaten and abandoned by God, turn to the

Second Letter of Paul to the Corinthians and read in the first chapter, beginning at the eighth verse:

For we do not want you to be ignorant, brethren, of the affliction we experienced in Asia; for we were so utterly, unbearably crushed that we despaired of life itself. Why, we felt that we had received the sentence of death; but that was to make us rely not on ourselves but on God who raises the dead; he delivered us from so deadly a peril, and he will deliver us; on him we have set our hope that he will deliver us again.

Blessed is the man who has learned in the furnace of his own experience that God gives grace to the weak and lifts up the downfallen.

So expect that a chart of your spiritual growth will resemble, if you remain faithful, a course something like the line of the national economy in recent years: a little up, a little down, a sharp rise, and a leveling off—inflation of spirit, recession of spirit—but in the long sweep, progress and growth. A person learning how to drive a car with a manual shift jerks, stops, slams into reverse, and only in the course of time learns to move from one gear to another smoothly. So you may grow, making two steps ahead, falling back one, but by God's grace keeping faithful in the way. We are reminded: "Some run swiftly, some walk; some creep painfully, but everyone who keeps on will reach the goal."

Conversion matures by growth. The goal of Christian life is maturity in Christ. What is this maturity in Christ? Paul gives a list of the things the mature Christian will cast aside, and then a list of the things the mature Christian will do and be. First, these are the things we must get rid of: ". . . immorality, impurity, licentiousness, idolatry, sorcery, enmity, strife, jealousy, anger, selfishness, dissension, party spirit, envy, drunkenness, carousing . . ." (Galatians 5:19, 20).

Are you rid of all of these?

And here are the qualities we must put on: ". . . compassion, kindness, lowliness, meekness, and patience, forbearing one another and, if one has a complaint against another, forgiving each other; as the Lord has forgiven you, so you also must forgive. And above all these put on love, which binds everything together in perfect harmony. And let the peace of Christ rule in your hearts. . . . And be thankful" (Colossians 3:12–15).

Does this describe you?

But we have not yet fully plumbed the depths of maturity in Christ. It includes more than personal qualities reflecting the Spirit of Christ in us. The author of Colossians continues his description of maturity in Christ: "And whatever you do, in word or deed, do everything in the name of the Lord Jesus, giving thanks to God the Father through him" (Colossians 3:17).

Whatever you do! Do everything! All of life must come under the sovereignty and converting power of Christ. No doors can remain closed to Him; every thought and action must become captive to Him until He permeates the totality of our existence, extending our conversion into our business life, our neighborhood life, our financial life, our sex life, our political and national life, our international life. For God is content with nothing less than the conversion of the world, starting always with you and me, and spreading until the kingdoms of this world shall become the Kingdom of our Lord Jesus Christ.

To become a Christian is to begin to see the world through Christ-colored glasses; it is to ask, in every new decision, "What is God's will for me here and now?" It is to become involved headlong in the painful struggles of humanity. It takes the twentieth-century Christian full speed ahead into the terrible problems of race relations, of labor-management troubles, of war and peace. It takes us out of our armchairs into all the murky corners of suffering and injustice, and requires us to work there for the reconciliation of all men. As God came to abide with us in person in Jesus Christ, so we Christians must wholly identify ourselves with all men, that God's redemptive will may be done in us and through us. This is something of what it means to grow up in every way into Christ, until we arrive at real maturity.

Jesus put it in two words: "Be perfect" (Matthew 5:48).

Any sane man must know that he falls far short of this maturity in Christ. Whenever we are inclined to feel complacent in our commitment, we should compare our puny spiritual achievements with this standard. One of the strange aspects of growing in grace is that the more we grow, the more we discover the extent of our own sinfulness. Paul said, "I am the foremost of sinners" (I Timothy 1:15). Well, maybe, but we're right up there with him. Let us never forget that we come to the church, not because we are good, but because we are not good; we are a society of sinners, called to be saints. Christ came to save sinners and make saints. If with men this is impossible, with Him all things are possible. This is His purpose for us. Paul writes to us as well as to the Christians of Philippi: "And I am sure that he who began a good work in you will bring it to completion at the day of Jesus Christ" (Philippians 1:6).

Amen. Come Lord Jesus!

VI

Conversion Endures in Discipline

It is for discipline that you have to endure.

HEBREWS 12:7

While on a retreat for the men of a local church, one young man said to the retreat leader: "I seem to have reached a plateau in my religious life. I've stopped making progress, and what's worse, it doesn't really bother me very much."

That man expressed quite candidly a universal danger in the experience of growth into Christ. There comes this time, after one has been awakened to decision for Christ, and by grace been empowered to grow toward maturity in Christ, when he reaches a plateau. What happens next is crucial. The whole enterprise hangs in the balance. One may put down roots which hold him fast and enable him to surge forward in growth. Or, and this happens to many, one may stop growing. One who has made a good start in the Christian life may lose interest, be sidetracked, and begin to coast, living off the principal of previous investment until one day he discovers he is bankrupt, having exhausted his spiritual resources. Such persons are not able to persevere; they have no spiritual stamina, no deep roots or anchor to windward. What can be done to help them and ourselves endure in conversion? The author of the Letter to the Hebrews provides the key to unlock the problem. In the eleventh chapter he gives stirring descriptions of courageous folk who remained steadfast in the faith through misfortune and adversity of every kind—Abraham, Moses, Gideon, Samson, David, the prophets. Then he opens the twelfth chapter in this way:

Therefore, since we are surrounded by so great a cloud of witnesses, let us also lay aside every weight, and sin which clings so closely, and let us run with perseverance the race that is set before us, looking to Jesus the pioneer and perfecter of our faith, who for the joy that was set before him endured the cross. . . . Consider him . . . so that you may not grow weary or faint-hearted. . . . It is for discipline that you have to endure.

Conversion endures in discipline. We are called to discipline ourselves that conversion may endure. "Discipline" has the same root meaning as "disciple." A disciple is a learner, one in training. Discipline is treatment suitable for a learner or one in training. Discipline is drill in the habits of obedience. The Christian is a soldier of Christ, being trained, fitted for combat, prepared for competition against a powerful enemy. Paul wrote the young Timothy: "Train yourself in godliness" (I Timothy 4:7).

The converted must be trained in godliness, equipped for the work of the ministry. All spiritual fat must be cut off. We must get in shape and stay in shape. The fact that a man was physically strong ten years ago does not guarantee his continuing strength today. The fact that once one was living a disciplined life in fellowship with Christ matters nothing at all for the present unless he has stayed in this training and continued to grow into Christ. Conversion endures only in discipline.

At this point we must face some unpleasant facts about ourselves. We Americans do not like either the idea or the experience of discipline. In a speech given some time ago Adlai Stevenson said:

The United States has lost impetus and conviction because it has confused the free with the free and easy. If freedom means ease alone, if it means shirking the hard disciplines of learning, if it means evading the rigors and rewards of creative activity, if it means more expenditure on advertising than education, if it means life adjustment courses in the schools, if it means—worst of all—indifference or even contempt for all but athletic excellence, we may keep for a time the forms of free society, but its spirit will be dead.[1]

We of the liberal Protestant tradition have accommodated ourselves to the cultural climate of the free and easy. We have capitulated to our secular environment, so that there is no longer any marked difference in behavior or outlook upon life between the average church member and his unchurched neighbor. Millions of church members have the forms of godliness but not the spirit or the power. Why? We are no longer a disciplined people. We like to make excuses for our impotence and lack of discipline. We say: "We Protestants are free. We're not like the Roman Catholics. Nobody can tell us what to do! We accept no external authority or imposed discipline."

All of this is fine and healthy, so long as we then impose upon ourselves an internal discipline and authority. Unfortunately, the people who most often scorn and belittle Roman Catholics for the strict performance of their religious obligations are usually the least disciplined in their own religious habits.

Or we say: "We musn't be overpious or pharisaical in our religious habits." This is a good word of caution, which has been underscored by the person who said: "Never allow yourselves to despise those who do not follow your rules of life, but force your hearts to love and pray for them. Let humility always be whispering into your ears that you yourselves would fall from those rules tomorrow if God should leave you to your own strength and wisdom."

Having recognized that pharisaism is a very real temptation for any person who takes the Christian life seriously, let us face the fact that this is not the problem for most contemporary church members. Our present danger is that of laxity, self-indulgence, and the rejection of all authority and discipline. And the plain truth is, only the disciplined change the world.

Whittaker Chambers describes the disciplined life of the underground Communist in the America of some thirty years ago. "Underground workers were absolutely forbidden to drink. . . . after the fashion of Communist friends, we all shared our lodgings, our food, our money, and even our clothes."[2] Typically, underground workers belonged to a study group that met once a week. It was not unusual for members of such groups to give ten per cent of their personal income to the Party.[3]

Isn't that kind of discipline amazing? Doesn't it sound like something out of the second chapter of Acts? And isn't the point clear? Thirty million Communists could take world leadership away from more than eight hundred million Christians, because they are disciplined, totally committed. How many new members would we receive into our churches if these were the conditions of membership? How many people would be left in our churches if that sort of rigorous discipline were required for continued membership? Would you be left?

What can we do about the exceedingly nominal membership of most of our church members? John Wesley was in the habit of purging the Methodist Societies of nominal members. All through his *Journal* there are references to this practice. The entry for Monday, June 18, 1744, reads: "The next day we endeavored to purge the society of all that did not walk according to the Gospel. By this means we reduced the number of members to less than nineteen hundred. But number is an inconsiderable circumstance. May God increase them in faith and love!"[4]

The tests applied for purging were not doctrinal beyond the central affirmations common to all Christians. Habits and behavior which Wesley deemed unfitting for the earnest Christian were questioned.[5] But the significant fact is that members were purged. Wesley was less impressed with numbers and more impressed with quality of commitment than are many of his twentieth-century followers. He wrote: "The society, which for the first year consisted of above 800 members, is now reduced to 400. But, according to the old proverb, the half is more than the whole. We shall not be ashamed of any of these when we speak with our enemies in the gate."[6]

A purge of local churches is not being suggested for our situation. But we are reminded that in the times when the church has been used powerfully by the Holy Spirit, numbers have not been great, but the quality of commitment has been deep. We are certain that the meaning and conditions of membership in the church must be re-examined and stiffened. We are convinced that the hope of the church in our time is the forging within each local church of a core of persons who are awakened and growing disciples of Christ. We contend that concerned Christians, whether laymen or ministers, must work with the few who are chosen among the many who are called, the few who are willing to pay the price of continuing discipleship, who will look for the narrow gate and seek to walk through it. We hope that the few who are chosen may be as leaven in the lump of the many who are called. We know that both individual and corporate conversion endure only in the disciplined life.

What are these disciplines whereby conversion may endure? They are not new. Twenty-five hundred years ago Jeremiah urged his people to "ask for the ancient paths" (Jeremiah 6:16). These holy habits are as old as bread for hunger and water for thirst. The man who thinks he has no need of them is either naive or foolish. We may call these disciplines *grooves of grace* which, when dug deep, become channels to release God's power for living the new life in Christ. Any listing of such grooves of grace must be arbitrary. Yet a growing Christian must have some habits of obedience by which to live. Prospective members of Aldersgate Church are invited to undertake a sixfold discipline, that their conversion may endure. Let us consider these disciplines, or grooves of grace.

The first groove of grace is *corporate worship.* The first obligation of the Christian as a member of the believing community, the Body of Christ, is to worship God. It must amaze the newcomer to the average church to discover that the church cares less about his weekly attendance than does his Service Club which regularly checks up on him. Anyone who regards his attendance at Sunday worship as an optional matter depending upon whim, fancy, or personal convenience, is not seriously interested in the new life with Christ. To be a Christian is to be a living member of the Body of Christ, whose characteristic action is the communal worship of the God and Father of our Lord Jesus Christ.

There is an objective reality about corporate worship, independent of our subjective wishes and rationalizations. If one wants to see the Rocky Mountains he must go to the West where they are! If one wants to live the new life with Christ he must gather with Christ's people for the administration of the sacraments and the preaching of the Word. God in His wisdom and mercy has established Baptism as that event in which we are grafted into the Body of Christ, and Holy Communion as that event in which we are sustained and nourished in the Body of Christ. God has given us the written Word which is offered to us through preaching in corporate worship. God has established the conditions and circumstances of Christian worship. One who would live the new life in Christ has no alternative to accepting and personally entering into these circumstances of Christian worship.

The second groove of grace is *daily prayer.* We need God's guidance and power every day. To forgive a hostile person today, we need power today. To make decisions according to God's will today, we need guidance today. Apart from Him, we can do nothing. A friend once said: "It isn't what I am *with* daily prayer; it's what I am *without* it!"

And that's the point. Without daily prayer, we operate on our own, and we soon find our spiritual resources depleted. Paderewski, the great Polish pianist, used to say that if he stopped practicing for one day, he noticed it. If he stopped practicing for two days, his family noticed it. If he stopped for three days, the public could tell the difference. If one stops practicing the presence of God in prayer regularly, he finds his heart becoming cool, his spirit insensitive to the needs of those about him, the wells of his compassion drying up, the urgency of his mission in the world subsiding. Often, he who perseveres through the desert spaces of his prayer life will come upon the oasis. A young woman who began to ask, seek, and knock earnestly, wrote to her minister:

> I had been on this daily prayer experiment (frankly a lot of reading and a little prayer), but felt this was strictly a one-way communication, and wasn't on a level I had been led to expect . . . until one afternoon I was kneeling, as usual "babbling away," and suddenly became aware of a feeling of over-flowing love. I could describe it only by saying it was something like a parent picking up a hurt child in his arms and saying "hush." (Be still and know that I am God comes pretty close to it.) Anyhow, I know God is real and that He loves me.

This firsthand knowledge of the presence and power of God came because she engaged in the discipline of daily prayer, and continued in that discipline. Conversion of the life of prayer endures in discipline.

The third groove of grace is *Bible reading and study.* Scores of people personally known to the writer have found that the Word of God becomes to them a Living Word spoken to their condition. The Bible provides the divine corrective for our private religious opinions. It keeps driving us from our word to the Word. Many people will come to know God only when they have first come to know about God. We grow in the knowledge of God as we expose ourselves to the events in which He has revealed Himself, as recorded in the Bible. This groove of grace is of crucial significance for the growth of the Christian in our day. The majority of our church members are biblically illiterate. They can tell a few biblical stories and recite several ethical maxims, but they know little of the mighty God who wielded the creative power, ruled the nations in judgment and mercy, spoke through the prophets, and came to save the world in Christ and establish His people by the Holy Spirit. How can one love God with one's mind if one does not have firsthand knowledge of the Bible? (Chapter IX will stress in greater detail the necessity of Bible study as a means of grace for our time.)

These first three grooves of grace are ways in which we open ourselves to receive grace from God. The remaining ones are ways in which we share with others the grace given us.

The fourth groove of grace is the *giving of money*. We discover, like the Good Samaritan, that loving our neighbor requires tangible financial help. The world, which is our neighbor, suffers in poverty and need. Most of us cannot go personally to minister to these needs—though some of us may be called to do this. But all of us can give money to meet the need. New Testament foundation for "proportional" giving, and more than proportional giving, may be found in the Second Letter of Paul to the Corinthians. He writes concerning the generosity of the Macedonian churches: "For they gave according to their means, as I can testify, and beyond their means, of their own free will" (II Corinthians 8:3).

Increasing numbers of Christians are accepting the practice of tithing as a discipline with implicit New Testament foundation. Jesus said to the leaders of the churches in His time: "Woe to you, scribes and Pharisees, hypocrites! for you tithe mint and dill and cummin, and have neglected the weightier matters of the law, justice and mercy and faith; these you ought to have done, without neglecting the others" (Matthew 23:23).

There is no question about the fact that many hardheaded businessmen, relatively impervious to the church's insistence on worship and prayer and Bible study, are first struck by the church's demand for sacrificial giving. A man in his thirties wrote to his minister not long ago:

As you know this is a monetary world. My background is one of trying to find peace of mind, enjoyment, and security through the accumulation of dollars. Since I was never able to accumulate enough, life tasted pretty flat, though I had much for which to be thankful. Inadvertently, my high esteem for the dollar did lead me closer to God. Two years ago I was asked to assist in the pledge drive. You will recall we were hitting hard for the new church building fund. Before I was to go out to ask others to pledge, our pledge card was given to me for completion. We had never signed a pledge before, and this one wasn't asking for change! I wrestled with it in my mind for a couple of days. Sure I wanted to do the right thing. We were expecting a baby in two months; maybe this would serve as a sort of bribe that all would go well. Business for me was good and looked better for the next year. Besides it might be thought I couldn't afford it. I signed. [Diogenes would have been pleased with this man!]

I attended church irregularly the next few months until it occurred to me that this was like paying for a new car and then letting it sit without using it. As my attendance grew more regular, I became aware of other men in the congregation who were apparently getting more from their church-going than I. They weren't holier-than-thou characters; they were men of my age, regular guys, neighbors in the community I'd known for some time.

This man and his wife began to take the Christian life very seriously. Each entered a prayer group; both went on retreats; both entered a Bible Study Group together. They grew! His letter continues:

We have since increased our pledge, though we are not yet tithing. Until we are tithing, we will not feel we are giving just return for that which the Lord has given us. I feel intensely now that fulfilling one's obligation to tithe plays an important part in his religious growth.

This man will discover that tithing does not exhaust his obligation, that when we have done *all*, we remain unworthy servants. But he has had the honesty to admit to himself that commitment which matters includes sacrificial giving of money.

The fifth groove of grace is *service*. To be a sinner means to be concerned with serving oneself. In popular parlance this is called "looking out for Number 1." This is where we all start. We begin as sinners viewing all things in terms of their effect on our desires and interests. Christ calls us to a life of serving others. He said: "For the Son of man also came not to be served but to serve" (Mark 10:45).

He showed us what He meant by taking the menial job of washing the feet of His friends after a long and dusty journey (John 13). According to Matthew, Jesus portrays the Last Judgment by indicating the righteous as those who have served the least of their fellows, and the unrighteous as those who have not served them (Matthew 25). The Protestant idea of vocation is that every Christian is called to serve God through his work and all his relationships. There is no division of sacred and secular calling. One's job is meant to be a major vehicle of one's ministry.

The calling to serve involves the housewife in ministry to her husband and children, and then to the needs of her neighborhood and community. The calling to serve involves the wage earner in ministry to his fellow workers, customers, and merchants. Some churches are currently holding vocational study groups in an attempt to help Christians understand and carry out their specific ministries through their daily work. One who is called to serve will take a different view of his leisure time from that of a person who is simply interested in indulging himself. The church must help her people work out an approach to leisure which is in keeping with the Christian's stewardship of time and talents. Even more important, the church must learn how to bring forth in her people the desire to serve (see Chapter XI).

The sixth groove of grace is witness. The author of Psalm 66 gives us a good definition of "witness":

> Come and hear, all you who fear God,
> and I will tell what he has done for me.

Most church people shrink from any kind of personal testimony. If a poll were taken in which persons were asked to place in order of priority these six disciplines of Christian life, there is little doubt that "witness" would come last. People are embarrassed and afraid of being regarded as religious fanatics. They do not know how to share their faith effectively, and for this the church must bear the blame. The church has not called her people to witness, nor trained her people for witness. Yet Jesus says to all Christians, ". . . you shall be my witnesses" (Acts 1:8).

No Christian can avoid or evade this indicative which becomes an imperative when Jesus says, "Go . . . and make disciples" (Matthew 28:19). The church must help her people grow in faith, so that they have some personal knowledge to share. The desire to witness comes only out of personal experience of God's grace.

A major concern of this book is to indicate one of the ways in which we can lead our people into such personal, firsthand knowledge of God's grace. The particular strategy to be suggested is *koinonia* groups (see Chapter IX). There is no question that the witness of laymen is the most powerful weapon in the church's arsenal. It was this lay witness as described in Acts that was the strength of the early church. It is lay witness which promises a renewal of the church in our time. As laymen take up their ministry and go to witness in the church and in the world, only then does the church begin to recover her mission.

These are six disciplines whereby conversion may endure. Growing Christians discover that they need one another for the living of this disciplined life. We know that we cannot travel this road alone. We know that we need the sustaining power of fellowship in Christ. As the author of the Letter to the Hebrews says: ". . . let us consider how to stir up one another to love and good works, not neglecting to meet together, as is the habit of some, but encouraging one another" (Hebrews 10:24, 25).

VII

Conversion Takes Place in Koinonia

> And they devoted themselves to the apostles' teaching and fellowship, to the breaking of bread and the prayers.
>
> Acts 2:42

Everybody is having fellowship these days. Service clubs, sewing circles, poker clubs, churches—all have fellowship. The word "fellowship" conveys various meanings to various people: coffee and doughnuts, beer and pretzels, the backyard fence, the bridge table, the cocktail party, the church supper. The great word "fellowship" is used to describe so many forms of human association that its meaning has become degraded into mere gregariousness, of a hail-fellow-well-met-and-soon-forgot nature.

So when we of the church try to explain what we mean by "Christian fellowship" we have to qualify and enlarge the term to fit the experience. We speak of the redemptive fellowship, the fellowship of the concerned, the fellowship of sharing, caring, and bearing. Our language strains awkwardly to express what we know. It may help us to turn to the only single word in any language which can convey the meaning of Christian fellowship. This is the word *koinonia*. It is the Greek word in the New Testament which is usually translated by "fellowship." A familiar phrase in which it is used is the Pauline benediction: "The grace of the Lord Jesus Christ, the love of God, and the fellowship [*koinonia*] of the Holy Spirit be with you all" (II Corinthians 13:14).

Normally it is not helpful to use words or terms of other languages in attempting to understand our faith. But in this instance we have much to gain and little to lose. *Koinonia* is fellowship with the triune God. It is fellowship "with the Father and with

65

his Son Jesus Christ" (I John 1:3). It is the fellowship of the
Holy Spirit, fellowship in Christ. It is fellowship in which the
sharers partake of a unique *esprit de corps* (spirit of a body);
the *esprit* is the Holy Spirit, the *corps* is the Body of Christ. Perhaps the best way of unfolding its meaning is to give some ex-
amples of *koinonia*.

My earliest experience of *koinonia* was in my home. Ours was
a loving home and family, like most; but the love was peculiarly
and wonderfully a love in Christ. Our fellowship together as
children and parents was a fellowship of the Holy Spirit. When
we had meals together, we began by holding hands around the
table and thanking God in Christ for our blessings. Before scatter-
ing to the duties of the day, we gathered together for family devotions. We repeated psalms together from memory. Each one
took his turn in reading Scripture and leading in prayer. We sang
a hymn and then knelt for the Lord's Prayer. As we grew up and
left home, letters would come in which our parents assured us of
their prayers for us, morning and night, in which they encouraged
us to know and love Christ. They introduced us to *koinonia*, fellowship in Christ. And I know this was the greatest gift they gave
to us. They loved us in Christ, and drew forth from us the capacity to be loved and to love. They hollowed out in us the
earthen vessels in which the treasure of Christ's presence could
be known. All the time, we were being converted, breathing the
aroma of Christ into our souls. It is no coincidence that the three
boys in our home all entered the Christian ministry. It was almost
inevitable, granting the *koinonia* which was ours from childhood.
For conversion takes place in *koinonia*.

Last winter a group of twenty-two men from our church went
on a weekend retreat at Shadybrook Retreat House near Cleveland. It was a new experience for all. The change of pace from
daily routine was startling. The men shared in discussion, corporate silence, singing and worship, Communion. Gradually a group
of individuals entered into a fellowship in which each was en-
riched and enriching. This was a fellowship new and fresh and
awakening. The men discovered that they were engaged in a common search for God, and a deep fellowship of common need was
known. One man said, "The boat I thought I was in alone, I
found to be crowded." The last evening they gathered in a small

room of the house. The room had been converted into a chapel. They sat in silence and one by one the men went forward to the altar. The rest prayed for those who were at the altar, and in turn were prayed for when kneeling themselves. Several days later one man said, "I felt closer to God in that moment than at any time in my life. It was a feeling . . . well . . . almost of love for one another." Another man said, "Out there I felt clean all over. We were a group of men together for two days on the highest level of conversation and sharing. I feel laundered and fresh." For many of those men, this was a transforming interlude, an awakening, a coming to decision. For they shared in *koinonia*, and conversion takes place in *koinonia*.

Four of the five Bible Study Groups in Aldersgate Church meet without the minister. One such group has been meeting for more than two years. Some time ago a sermon was preached in church on *koinonia*. The next week a letter came from a person in that Study Group. It reads:

I wish you could have been hidden away in our apartment last night. For I think you would have been as thrilled with our Bible Study group meeting as I was. There was much discussion and a real sharing of beliefs, interpretations and personal theologies. And in addition our group really experienced your Sunday sermon *koinonia*. There was that indefinable "something" present, making us a true unity as a group, and not simply a collection of individuals physically in the same room for three hours. The "why" of all this happening last night I don't know. Partly the lesson material itself, I think. We were studying John 17—20 and especially in the prayer of John 17 did we find inspiration and the very bases of our own faith today. We were all struck by John's description of the oneness of man with God and Jesus, and through them his oneness with his fellow-believers. Here again was your *koinonia* in our lesson, and in practice in our group. I thought you would be pleased to hear that as a group we are growing toward God through Christ and in fellowship one with another.

The people in that group are ten in number. They have a wide variety of abilities and interests. In the context of Bible study and prayer, they have entered into a new dimension of friendship, the fellowship of the Holy Spirit, *koinonia*. And they are being changed; for conversion takes place in *koinonia*. Recently one of the couples in that group moved away from Cleveland. The group held a special meeting for them. We shared dinner around a large table; a book inscribed with the words of our love for them and signed by the members of the group was given to them; Communion was shared around the table. It was an evening of fellowship long to be remembered. Soon afterward, a letter came from the couple thus feted. It read:

Chuck and I were greatly surprised and deeply moved by your tangible tribute on our behalf to our Bible Study Group's very special *koinonia*. Leaving it and all of you is going to make one of the deepest holes in all of our move away—a hole we will never be able to fill again in quite the same way. We shall treasure your book with its lovely inscription and all of your signatures as well as our memories of Monday night with its deep fellowship, touching prayers—and our usual gay fun. Many, many thanks.

Shortly before the Christmas season one year, a young woman in one of our Bible Study Groups felt the understanding and love of the other persons in the group, with the result that she was released to share a painful experience with others for the first time. She told us that her family had lived in two rooms behind a bar. When she was a child of six, she happened to come through the curtain separating the bar from the living area just in time to overhear her parents talking about divorce. Her father said to her mother: "I don't want Jean. Girls are expensive to bring up. We'll have to do something else with her." As a six-year-old child she discovered that her father didn't want her, didn't really love her. Her home was broken up, and the mark was real upon her. She said as she told us of the experience: "You see why Christmas means so much to me and always has. Because it is the assurance that God, my Father in heaven, loves me so much He came to be with me in Christ on that first Christmas." For all of us present, this was a deeply felt sharing and joy in the presence of God, the *koinonia* of the Holy Spirit. *Koinonia* is healing friendship in which we are converted.

The first time a small group of Christian friends shared Holy Communion in a particular woman's home, she was moved to write:

The circle of my life was complete when my friends, my dearest friends, prayed and shared Communion in our home. Myself, my family and home, and my friends are now intertwined in God's love. I've known heaven on earth and am slowly becoming aware of what lies ahead. I feel this is just a beginning, a step toward growth.

Heaven on earth. God present with us in Christ. This is *koinonia*, that communion in which He abides in us and we in Him. This is the communion of the saints which partakes of eternity in the here and now. It is that communion in which conversion takes place.

Is it a bit clearer what *koinonia* is and means? *Koinonia* is always the context of conversion, the fellowship in which lives are changed by Christ. No one is converted by himself; still less is one able to keep growing by himself. You may have observed that every instance of *koinonia* cited was *koinonia* shared in a small group: a family, a group of twenty-two men, three Bible Study Groups. *Koinonia* requires personal participation and mutual sharing with others. This is possible only in small groups. In the words of Lewis Mumford:

> No matter how inclusive the province of any association or institution, whether it be a trade union or a church or a bank, there must be at the central core an organic form of association; a group small enough for intimacy and for personal evaluation, so that its members can meet frequently as a body and know each other well, not as units, but as persons: small enough for direct face-to-face meeting, for discussion and decision on the basis of intimate understanding.[1]

It is no coincidence that there were 12 disciples, not 120 or 1200, but 12—a small group of men with whom Jesus could share deep fellowship.

John Wesley discovered the necessity of the small-group fellowship for conversion and continuing growth into Christ. The Class Meeting of the early Methodists provided a context for mutual encouragement and sharing of faith and love. Each new convert automatically became a member of such a class which met weekly to pray, study the Bible, seek guidance from one another, and grow in grace. Six years after the start of such Class Meetings, Wesley commented:

> It can scarce be conceived what advantages have been reaped. . . . Many now happily experienced that Christian fellowship of which

they had not so much as an idea before. They began to "bear one
another's burdens," and naturally to "care for each other." As they
had daily a more intimate acquaintance with, so they had a more en-
deared affection for, each other. And "speaking the truth in love,
they grew up into him in all things."[2]

In 1743, reference was made to the Class Meeting in the General Rules as a distinctive feature of Methodism.

The fellowship of the class meeting was undoubtedly one of the
most precious things in the lives of the first two generations of Methodists. Their love for the little circles to which they belonged led
them to endure all kinds of physical hardship that they might enjoy
it.[3]

Another commentator wrote:

It was in these meetings, rather than in the preaching services
where the great majority of conversions occurred.[4]

This has been precisely my own experience. I have watched
proportionately more lives genuinely converted in and through
small groups meeting for prayer, Bible study, and the sharing of
life than in the usual organizations and activities of the institutional church. Those who penetrate into the inner core of the
life of a local church will sometimes find and know *koinonia*
apart from such a small-group experience. The great majority of
people who are not "on the inside" will come into *koinonia* only
in the small group. In such a group, those who are awakened in
a time of grace will be confirmed in decision, encouraged to grow,
and enabled to abide in discipline.

It should be noted that smallness in and of itself is no guarantee of *koinonia*. Those groups in which *koinonia* is known are
usually doing and sharing quite specific things together. We could
take as a norm for the sharing of *koinonia* the practice of the
early Christians as described in the second chapter of Acts, especially verse 42: "And they devoted themselves to the apostles'
teaching and fellowship, to the breaking of bread and the prayers."

The Apostles' teaching was the witness of those who had
known Jesus or heard firsthand stories about Him. It was also the
spelling out of the Christian way of life. Some of this teaching
has been recorded in the New Testament. Today the Apostles'

teaching means Bible study, especially study of the New Testament.

The Apostles' fellowship was a total sharing of life, later described in Acts as including economic sharing. It was a genuine family in Christ.

The breaking of bread was the sharing of Communion, the distinctive Christian act of worship from the very beginning in the early church. Celebrated on Sunday, the day of the resurrection of Christ, this Communion highlighted the presence of the risen Christ as well as re-enacting the death of Jesus, and it looked forward to the communion of the saints in the Kingdom of God.

The prayers included the shared prayer life of fellow believers.

Bible study, sharing of life, Communion, prayer—here are the ingredients which again and again are found to provide the context for koinonia. They could almost be described as the conditions for koinonia.

The implications of this for the modern church are clear. Conversion takes place in koinonia. Therefore, the church must foster and sustain the conditions in which koinonia can be known. This cannot be done for most people simply through morning worship. Worship is indispensable as the weekly meeting of the Christian community. But it is effective only as the total sharing of all the people of the friendship in Christ they have known between Sundays. There cannot be real firsthand koinonia among hundreds of people. The best evidence of this is the fact that hundreds of people in a given local church can worship faithfully for years without any appreciable change in quality of commitment or direction of life. Many of the same people, exposed to a breath or taste of koinonia in some small group, begin to change in a matter of months. The church is obligated to lead its people into small-group fellowship where the conditions for koinonia prevail.

The Church's ministry is always a ministry of preparation, of getting people ready for the coming of the Spirit, of fulfilling the conditions for koinonia. Norman Cousins, editor of the Saturday Review, some time ago described what he calls the "moment of triumph" in the experience of an author:

This is when an important idea is born, when there is a sudden glorious clicking in the vitals of the writer, when he knows that his creative wells are full and demanding release. It is also a moment of commitment, for the writer knows that the idea will possess him and hover over him until he puts down the words that will set him free again.

Can it happen to anybody? It can happen only to a person who is ready for it. The creative process depends least of all upon accident. It requires that the mind be properly worked and tended.

Albert Schweitzer, paddling upstream in a canoe on the River Ogouwe, perceived an island in the middle of the river, and there occurred to him the idea of "reverence for life." Did the island produce the idea? If so, the same idea should have occurred to everyone who saw the island under similar circumstances. This moment of creative triumph occurred to Albert Schweitzer because he was ready for it, because his moral imagination had been cultivated as carefully and painstakingly as a farmer his fields.[5]

One is awakened to decision when he is ready for it, when he has been asking, seeking, and knocking.

The church should always be helping people plow the ground or hoist the sail, making ready for the gift of seed or wind. True, nothing the church does can invoke the Holy Spirit or guarantee His coming. He converts lives wherever and whenever they are converted. But He uses us in the church to help people become ready. Ours is a John the Baptist ministry of preparing the way for the One who will come after us. We are called to create the conditions for conversion within the church.

VIII

The Imperative: Conversion within the Church[1]

For the time has come for judgment to begin with
the household of God.

I PETER 4:17

We live in the heyday of successful evangelism. For psycho-
logical and historical reasons the cultural climate in our time is
favorable to religion. Magazine and book publishers, Hollywood
producers, and some ministers have discovered the salability of
the religious product. And so the church is popular today in a
way that it was not twenty-five or thirty years ago, and as it probably will not be some years hence. People flock to our churches,
buildings are built, budgets go up, numbers mount, attendance
increases, and without much thought we gladly regard these facts
as marks of the Kingdom of God in our midst.

There are two major types of evangelism which have produced
the tide of new members rolling into the churches. One is the
"hard-sell" approach: Madison Avenue with a halo; anything
goes so long as they join up. Two years ago in an evangelistic
campaign, a big successful church instructed its laymen to go to
people who had never been in their church before and say to
them, "Come this Sunday, join next." And they racked up impressive totals of new members in that campaign.

This hard-sell evangelism reminds me of a description of the
practice of head-hunting in an excellent book on evolution, *Man's
Emerging Mind*, by the English biologist N. J. Berrill. He writes:

In taking a head the spirit within is captured, and a collection of
heads adds to the general stock of spirit or soul matter belonging to
a community. Head-hunting, like cannibalism, is in essence a religious
practice, complimentary to the victim even if not enjoyed by him.[2]

73

The idea is, you see, that each new head strengthens the community. Spiritual head-hunting survives in our day in the modern church as a capitulation to the overwhelming stress of our culture on success, a success always measured in terms of numbers and dollars. We talk about the new members we have "taken in," and we may be speaking deeper truth than we realize.

The other contemporary type of evangelism we may call the "soft-soap" approach. This is the peace-of-mind-at-any-price school, the popular panacea religion which sells on the newsstands. An example of it is a bulletin put out by the Protestant Council of New York City, giving advice to its radio speakers:

> Subject matter should project love, joy, courage, hope, faith, trust, goodwill. Generally avoid criticism, controversy. In a very real sense we are "selling" religion. Therefore, training of Christians on cross-bearing, sacrifice, and service, calling sinners to repentance, these are out of place. As apostles can we not extend an invitation in effect: "Come and enjoy our privileges, meet good friends, see what God can do for you?"[3]

I seem to recall another sort of invitation: "If any man would come after me, let him deny himself and take up his cross and follow me" (Mark 8:34). These may be useful suggestions for radio and television, though evidently Billy Graham missed this bulletin. But the unhappy fact is that this is the soft-soap approach characteristic of the church's appeal in our time.

We succumb to this because we are afraid. We have to compete with all the lures of society and culture, and so we are afraid to present the gospel in its full dimension of judgment and grace. But we have been in error. A very perceptive layman in our church, personnel director of a large department store, once described his searching for the church in a sermon. He said:

> During the period I was outside the Church, I did make a couple of efforts to return. But the overtures the Church made to me were along these lines: Wonderful recreational programs; stimulating group discussions on current events; a place to meet nice girls. But this was a time in my life when I had all of the recreational activity I could handle. I wasn't interested in organizational discussions; nor was I interested in meeting nice girls. I knew one, and a few more, nice or not, would have complicated the situation. What I needed at the time was some good, sound, fundamental faith, and a real spiritual

overhauling. And deep down I knew I needed it, but what I got was a lot more reasons why I wasn't interested in the Church.

That man has now been in a Bible Study Group for two years; he started a luncheon prayer group; he has been the president of our Men's Organization. He needed strong red meat; the church offered him pablum. He was hungry; the church didn't feed him.

Now why do we do this sort of thing? Why do we sweep crowds of genial, attractive pagans into our churches without any adequate challenge? We justify it by making a fallacious assumption which an ecclesiastical leader made a while ago. He said: "I make no apology for my interest in statistics and the numbers of new members. Why, just think, every new member means another person engaged in daily prayer, another family sharing in family devotions, a man putting Christian ideals into practice in his work, and another marriage blessed by Christ." If it were only so! The fact is, in a local church less than one-third of the members engage in any kind of daily prayer; a majority of the members make an easy identification between Christian discipleship and the American Way of Life; and the overwhelming odds are that new people coming in will fall into the same pattern. Here is the nub of the fallacy: we say that church membership equals Christian discipleship. One church member equals one disciple of Christ. But it is not so! How could it be so when the cross is gone from our invitation to church membership, when we accept anyone who can stand up on a Sunday morning and say "I will" at the proper time. Harry Golden, that piquant editor of the *South Carolina Israelite*, was quoted in *Life* magazine as saying this:

> If I were faced today with the decision my ancestors faced . . . become a Christian or die . . . I would pick a Church fast. There is nothing to offend me in the modern Church. The minister gives a talk on juvenile delinquency one week, reviews a movie next week, then everyone goes downstairs and plays Bingo. The first part of a Church they build nowadays is the kitchen. Five hundred years from now, people will dig up these Churches, find the steam tables, and wonder what kind of sacrifices we performed.[4]

The church has forgotten that it is supposed to be the leaven and not the lump. You know the old phrase: "Sometimes you have trouble getting the church into the world, and sometimes you have trouble getting the world out of the church." Our situation today is that we have trouble telling the difference between the church and the world. A perfect and appalling illustration of this capitulation to culture occurred not long ago in the building of a large church in a metropolitan area. The church was of Georgian style, and the question arose what to put on the top of the steeple. With no argument from anyone, it was decided not to put a cross on top but a weathervane because "the weathervane is more in keeping with the style of the architecture." And so the church in that community holds aloft as the symbol of its gospel, not a cross but a weathervane. The church has pulled the Trojan horse of secularism inside her own walls. "The time has come for judgment to begin with the household of God." How may we prepare for judgment that we may be ready for renewal?

The first thing to reaffirm is that we must stick with the church. As someone has remarked: "The church is like Noah's Ark; if it weren't for the storm outside, you couldn't stand the smell inside." There is a storm outside, and the church, pervaded as it is with the smell of genial paganism, is still the ark of salvation, and there is no other.

The second thing to reaffirm is that by ourselves we cannot do anything about it. We as men are powerless to start revivals. We cannot schedule or blueprint or conjure into being the reviving Spirit of God. The Holy Spirit, like the wind, comes when and where He wills. So, with men, it is impossible.

The third thing to reaffirm is that with God all things are possible. And in fact, the most exciting truth of our generation is that God has already started something! This is the tremendous experience we are having in our different churches, and in different ways. The Holy Spirit is loose again in the world; lives are changing; the church is being reborn and renewed in place after place; a new Pentecost as of the days of the early church is at hand. So our privilege and obligation are not to start a revival; rather, to watch for the tide rolling in, to catch it, to seek to ride with it, and to make new channels for these rivers of grace. We are to be instruments for the Holy Spirit who is awakening us and breathing His power into our sleeping churches. Quite specifically, it is the job of Christian laymen and ministers to create the conditions for conversion within the life of the local church. It is God who converts lives; it is we who are called to create the conditions of conversion.

A friend once said to me after I had bemoaned all the superficial reasons which brought people to church: "Look, quit worrying about why they come. Your job is to do something with them when they do come." And he was right, of course. I believe we must begin to do something quite specific and challenging at the point of church membership. The funnel must be narrowed there. Institutional evangelism, winning people to join the local church, is all right only when it is immediately followed by new-member training and preparation in which persons are challenged to commit themselves to Jesus Christ. Membership in the church is meant to be the outer symbol of inner commitment to Jesus Christ. Evangelism outside the church, evangelism in breadth, is essential. But what is even more crucial in our time is evangelism inside the church, evangelism in depth. The church is loaded with nominal members—genial, friendly folk who are ignorant of the Bible and innocent of disciplined Christian commitment. They are sincerely but superficially Christian. This order of Christianity is drawn in pastel. Its faith is shallow; its people are without any spiritual history; they are not growing; they are spiritually asleep. The time has come for judgment to begin with the household of God.

The imperative for our time is conversion within the church.

IX

The Strategy: Koinonia Groups

Let us consider how to stir up one another to love
and good works, not neglecting to meet together,
. . . but encouraging one another.

HEBREWS 10:24, 25

The average American family moves once every five years. This
population mobility heightens the urgency of the church's task
of converting the vast ranks of her uncommitted people. The
church must learn how to reach her people both quickly and
deeply. The time is short. The time will come, historically speaking, when going to Church is no longer the popular, respectable
thing to do. The froth now merrily bubbling at the surface of the
church's life will disappear, and only those who deeply care will
remain. Strategies change with changing circumstances. The author of the Letter to the Hebrews raises the question of strategy
and poses the answer in one sentence: "Let us consider how to
stir up one another to love and good works, not neglecting to
meet together . . . but encouraging one another." We stir up
one another to the new life in Christ by meeting together and
encouraging one another. A small group is necessary for this kind
of personal and mutual encouragement. The strategy for our time
is the small-group approach. We must train a hard core of committed and growing disciples who shall serve as leaven within the
local church.

We have ample biblical authority for the training of such a
hard core. This is precisely what Jesus did with the twelve disciples. We read in the eighth, ninth, and tenth chapters of the
Gospel according to Mark that Jesus took these closest friends
apart from the crowds and taught them the conditions of disciple-

ship. He was deliberately training them for leadership after His death. It wasn't the crowds to whom Jesus preached, but this little group of men that became the foundation of the early church. Paul preached to the crowds in synagogues, on public squares, wherever he could reach them; but it wasn't the crowds, it was the little groups of people in Galatia, in Philippi, in Corinth, with whom Paul lived and worked for several months at a time, which became the foundation of the Mediterranean churches.

Church history documents the same creative experience. It was the small monastic fellowships which produced the power to waken the church from the doldrums of the Dark Ages. We have seen in Chapter VII how John Wesley developed the Class Meeting as a way of awakening and sustaining the converts of the Methodist Revival in England. So it is no new thing, nor a coincidence, that today there is a return to the small-group fellowship within the church. It is a medium through which God has evidently chosen to work in powerful and permanent ways to help people start growing and continue to grow in Christ. In England one form of this approach is the "House-Church" movement described by E. W. Southcott in *The Parish Comes Alive.*[1] Another form, in Scotland, is outlined in *The Face of My Parish* by Tom Allan.[2] On the Continent, the Evangelical Lay Academies provide another illustration. In this country, a great variety of small groups is emerging within the life of the church. The Yokefellow movement with headquarters in Richmond, Indiana, is the catalyst and creator of hundreds of such groups. The book *Spiritual Renewal through Personal Groups* by John Casteel[3] describes a variety of such groups emerging in different churches.

These groups are variously described as personal groups, discovery groups, study groups. Perhaps the most common form of this small-group life is the prayer group, whose many expressions are described in the book *Two or Three Together* by Freer and Hall.[4] Recently a friend wrote: "I like to call them 'exposure groups' for the simple reason that these small groups seem to expose themselves to God, to the living Christ in their midst, to the New Testament and to one another's questions and problems." We are talking about exposure in a particular environment, that atmosphere which can be defined only as *koinonia*. The most concise and adequate term to describe the small-group life in its New Testament dimension is *koinonia*. For many people the terminology of "prayer" and "study" groups signifies limited and narrowed concerns. We are after nothing less than the new creation, the personal and corporate conversion which takes place in *koinonia*. The strategy for conversion within the church is *koinonia* groups. (Only recently have we settled on *koinonia* as the most adequate term to describe these groups. We have called them Bible Study Groups in Aldersgate Church. The reader will therefore understand that all references to Bible Study Groups in Aldersgate Church specify what from now on we shall term *koinonia* groups.)

Let it be acknowledged that no particular form of group meeting has a monopoly on the Holy Spirit. Let it also be declared that certain conditions seem uniquely propitious as preparation for the coming of the Holy Spirit. The four "conditions" for *koinonia* enumerated in Acts 2:42 (described here in Chapter VII) are: Bible study; deep sharing of faith and life; prayer; Holy Communion.

In most forms of the small group, prayer and the sharing of life are included. The sacrament of Holy Communion is the center of the small-group life in the House-Church movement in England. In addition, many non-Anglican Protestants are finding great meaning in the sharing of Communion in small groups. If any one of the four conditions for *koinonia* can be singled out as uniquely important for our time, it is Bible study. Bible study is crucial, not as an academic exercise in biblical facts, but as the concrete way in which uninformed persons may together seek the God of the Bible. Timothy, in the second letter written to him, is reminded of the importance of Bible study:

Remember . . . how from early childhood your mind has been familiar with the holy scriptures, which can open the mind to the salvation which comes through believing in Christ Jesus. All scripture is inspired by God and is useful for teaching the faith and correcting error, for resetting the direction of a man's life and training him in good living. The scriptures are the comprehensive equipment of the man of God, and fit him fully for all branches of his work. [II Timothy 3:15–17, Phillips]

There are at least three good reasons why Bible study must be at the core of *koinonia* groups. First, it is a matter of record that reappropriation of the biblical message has historically been integral to the significant awakenings or reformations in the history of the church. The Reformation, the Wesleyan movement in eighteenth-century England, the New England awakenings of the eighteenth century, and the current renewal of life within the Church are cases in point. It is also significant that individual awakenings have often occurred in the context of Bible study or reading. Among such would be included the names of St. Augustine, Martin Luther, the Wesley brothers, Jonathan Edwards, and a host of others. There is nothing magical about the Bible. But it is the written vehicle through which the Word in ever-fresh and powerful ways becomes the Living Word to our condition. It is the document of Christian faith and experience. Persons who would grow into Christian maturity are driven to study the Bible.

The second reason is that study of the Bible provides the determinative substance of the fellowship of the small group. Prayer groups or discovery groups can become self-centered and sentimental if there is no objective material on which to focus concern. The Bible provides the authoritative content of the faith, and there is special need in our time for a clarification and redefinition of the faith. Neglect of Biblical theology by the recent generation has left most of our people abysmally ignorant of Christian doctrine.

This was brought home forcefully to the writer in a recent retreat for people in both management and labor, as well as a few clergymen. The one thing we all had in common was that we were members of Christian churches. The purpose of the retreat was to discover whether we could consider some sort of "Christian approach" to the problems of labor-management relations. The clergymen present discovered how ineffectively the church has been communicating her gospel in recent years. For these laymen had an idea of Christian faith which they summed up in the phrase "Christian principles." They kept repeating, both labor and management people, that all we need to do is apply "Christian principles" and all our problems will be solved. Finally one of the laymen was asked to write on a blackboard a list of these principles. He did so. The list included the following: sincerity, integrity, honesty, fairness, consistency, mutual understanding.

These are all fine virtues, of course. But they are not specifically Christian principles. Any good Jew would adhere to this list and would justly resent the claim that these are "Christian" principles. Most of our nonchurched and non-Christian friends would subscribe to these principles. This is simply a list of virtues which any good citizen of a democracy would endorse, whatever faith or lack of faith he possessed. These laymen on the retreat had unconsciously boiled down Christianity to good citizenship. They were saying in effect: "Christianity equals decent, civilized behavior."

Now of course Christ isn't essential to decent, civilized behavior. And one of the laymen said as much by declaring that Christ wasn't necessary in this matter, that all we needed was a little more common sense. Our church laymen unwittingly came up with a definition of Christian faith which made Christ unnecessary.

As we talked further, the laymen backed away from using the word "sin." This was not a meaningful word to them. They understood it chiefly as a kind of negative thinking. Its remedy was positive thinking and a bit more moral effort on man's part. This of course neatly eliminated Christ as Savior, because there was no need for forgiveness, only for more human effort. The cross appeared to these men as merely a symbol, and a rather unfortunate and defeatist one at that. Leaders of the church need to face the fact that many of our leading laymen have this deistic, Unitarian idea of Christian faith. Only persons ignorant of the New Testament could confuse Christian faith with the diluted and emasculated version of the faith which these laymen had articulated. There is desperate need in our churches for firsthand study of the Bible.

The present generation has been occupying itself in the expansion of the church's membership. In time of such expansion there is always danger of diluting or distorting the faith to accommodate it to the cultural climate. Evidently Paul knew the same danger in the great expansion of that first century. He wrote to Timothy: "If you put these instructions before the brethren, you will be a good minister for Christ Jesus, nourished on the words of the faith and of the good doctrine which you have followed" (I Timothy 4:6). To Titus were written the words: "[One who would serve God] must hold firm to the sure word as taught, so that he may be able to give instruction in sound doctrine and also to confute those who contradict it" (Titus 1:9).

The word "doctrine" occurs in the letters to Timothy and Titus exactly fifteen times. It is imperatively now our task, as it was then their task, to make clear to our people just what Christian faith is, in contradistinction to all of the faiths and religions of the day. The point is not to get after heretics but to make clear where are the boundaries of heresy, to stake out the area of Christian faith, and to train people in that faith. This need not and should not imply any strait-jacket orthodoxy; but it does give prime importance to the quest for understanding the faith. It does bring to the fore the matter of loving God with our minds as well as our hearts. It does stress the fact that an important factor in persons coming to know God is their coming to know about Him. The Bible is essential for this purpose.

A third reason for Bible study as the center of koinonia groups is quite pragmatic. It is the best way to get large numbers of people into small groups. Prayer groups are often populated with the faithful, and the beginner feels too uncertain to come into such a group. Not every one can be expected, as a Christian, to be concerned with various forms of discovery groups. *Every mature Christian and everyone seeking to become a mature Christian can be expected to seek firsthand knowledge of the Bible as essential to his being a mature Christian!* The fact is, very few people within local churches do have anything resembling a firsthand knowledge or understanding of the Bible. People generally know this and feel uneasy about it. Many will respond to the invitation to join with others in Bible study, to grapple with questions and doubts which have lain submerged for years, to work out an intellectually respectable faith for themselves personally. In my experience, a great many people who would never venture into a prayer group will come as "seekers" into a Bible study group. The only conditions of entrance are an awareness that the Bible is uniquely important to the understanding and living of Christianity, and an honest desire to take a look at it with others.

We shall now relate the experience of Aldersgate Church with such *koinonia* groups centering on Bible study, an experience which has led us to the convictions enumerated above. While in seminary, my wife and I shared a devotional group fellowship with four other men and their wives. We shared this discussion, Bible study, and prayer for three years together, and unquestionably it was the most important factor in our spiritual growth during those years. We left seminary concerned to create this small-group fellowship in our parish ministry as soon as it seemed practicable.

We had been in Aldersgate Church a few months when a young couple with very little church background joined that church. The whole family, father and mother and three children, were baptized one Sunday morning. Shortly after joining the church they said, "We don't know anything about Christianity, but we'd like to learn about our faith. Can you help us?" This seemed to be the opening we had waited for. We found two other couples and two or three other individuals, and we began to meet twice a month at night in the homes of the people who were in the group.

We studied the Gospels; we discussed; we prayed together. The group went along without much organization, and we watched the friendships of those within the group begin to deepen. We were in one another's homes; we were talking about things that mattered. No matter how academically I would start the discussion, the people would invariably bring it down to their daily lives where they needed help. We began to see that this experience was providing real Christian fellowship, more fellowship in Christ than any other group or work going on in our church.

The group had its ups and downs. At one point interest seemed to flag and we were at the point of calling it quits. But gradually it began to grow, and within two years it was becoming too large for fruitful sharing. We tried to think of ways to start a new group, how and when to do it. You understand the frustrations of trying to get ahead of the Holy Spirit and plan His work ahead of time for Him. We met a blank wall everywhere we turned, and so we did nothing.

As it happened, we had been planning for several months a seminar for our Sunday School teachers. It consisted of four evening meetings on Christian Doctrine. This was the most amazing brief experience of the presence of the Holy Spirit which I have ever personally known. I was astounded by the hunger of these people to have personal firsthand experience of God's power and love. I didn't have any feeling at all that the Holy Spirit was working through me. I felt just the same as always, but I could see others changing, lives being awakened and transformed. The chairman of our Commission on Education later described this experience to our people gathered for the annual congregational meeting:

This course was undoubtedly, as many teachers witnessed, a genuine spiritual awakening for every one present. We all felt the refreshing presence of the Holy Spirit in our midst, actively working with us and through us, strengthening our faith in Jesus Christ, and renewing our desire to learn and do the will of God. The spiritual hunger was not satisfied [at the end of these meetings] and as a direct result of the feeling which grew out of the seminar, two new Bible Study Groups have been formed.

Several different groups have been started in this period of five years. Five groups are now meeting, involving about sixty people.

So much for the history of these groups. Now, for the procedure. We meet two evenings a month in the homes of members. This means that couples can and do share the experience together. Meeting in the home was more or less incidental in the beginning, but it has become an indispensable part of the whole fellowship experience. It takes the church out of the church building and into the places where people live.

The length of a meeting is normally two hours. We begin at 8:00 P.M. with a fifteen-minute period of devotions. One person or couple leads. There will be Scripture, a corporate silence of several minutes in which we can "center down" Quaker style, and prayer concluding with the Lord's Prayer. The discussion of the material studied lasts for an hour and a half. At the end there is a period of shared prayer. (See the last section of the next chapter for full details on the methods of discussion and the way in which prayer is shared.) On special occasions, such as the first group meeting in the fall, we share Communion together. Many find this intimate, informal Communion the most meaningful they have ever known.

Now to mention the materials we have used. At first our practice was haphazard, but we have learned what materials are fruitful, some that are not, and at least something about where to begin. Perhaps the briefest way of getting at this is to say what we now do with a beginning group. We set up a two-year cycle, that is: a course for a group meeting twice a month for nine months of the year, breaking off in the summer and starting up again in the fall. It will be clear that a group meeting every week could cover the same material in one year. It is best to start off with an introduction to the Bible or survey of the Bible, in which the ground can be cleared in the matter of literal interpretation. Such problems as, "The Bible says the world was created in six days; my science teacher said it was three billion years," can be dealt with. The best material we have found for this is Robert MacAfee Brown's book, *The Bible Speaks to You.*[5] Another excellent source is a little series of six pamphlets called *Consider the Bible.*[6]

Then we have studied the Gospel according to Mark. The best commentary available for the average layman is William Barclay's *The Gospel of Mark.*[7] We find that laymen are thrilled with it. It's like the exposition in the *Interpreter's Bible.* A few laymen will want to study; many more will be willing to read. Barclay's commentary allows them to read, and with great fruit. In conjunction with the Scripture, we have used a book in the Layman's Theological Library called *The Meaning of Christ* by Robert Johnson.[8] We read the Gospel itself and also a theological interpretation to provoke our discussion and understanding.

Then we read Acts, which laymen always find tremendously exciting. Here's where we come to the Holy Spirit. He's literally everywhere in Acts, and by this time the people in the group know that He is currently with them. Using J. B. Phillips' translation or Barclay's commentary, we read *The Significance of the Church* by R. M. Brown, also in the Layman's Theological Library.[9] So in that first year, we have studied an introduction to the Bible, the life, death, and resurrection of Christ, and the birth and growth of the early church.

The second year we study Paul's Letters. We have tried commentaries on the letters, such as those prepared by William Barclay; and we have also tried reading the letters in J. B. Phillips' translation, supplemented by additional nonbiblical books. We read Ephesians as the basis for our understanding of the nature and mission of the church. We are still searching for the right nonbiblical book to read in conjunction with Ephesians. We read Galatians as the foundation for a systematic theology; *The Faith of the Church* by James Pike and Norman Pittenger[10] and *The Faith of the Gospel* by Eric Osborn[11] have been useful as supplementary reading. We read First Corinthians as the basis for a formulation of Christian ethics. *Doing the Truth* by James Pike[12] and *Making Ethical Decisions* by Howard Kee[13] have been useful as supplementary reading. This completes a two-year cycle of study.

For those groups which continue, now on lay leadership, the possibilities are endless. One group which has had extensive experience with shared lay leadership has studied Genesis, the Fourth Gospel, some of the Psalms, and some of the Parables of Jesus. Commentaries used have included *The Interpreter's Bible*[14] and George Buttrick's *The Parables of Jesus*[15] in addition to Barclay's commentaries. So much for the history of these groups, and the procedures and materials used. Now let us relate the results of the koinonia groups as we have observed them and shared in them over these five years.

X

New Creation in the Church: Changing Lives

> Therefore, if any one is in Christ, he is a new cre-
> ation; the old has passed away, behold, the new has
> come.
>
> II CORINTHIANS 5:17

It is right that we should look for and expect results in our work in the church. Paul wrote to the Romans: ". . . I should like to see some results among you, as I have among other Gentiles" (Romans 1:11; Phillips).

These results may or may not be subject to statistical analysis. They are in the realm of changed and changing lives. And this is in fact the chief result or outcome of these *koinonia* groups. In this context scores of lives have been touched by the Holy Spirit; many have been genuinely and permanently converted to Christ. We are beholding new creation in the church. We know in our own experience the validity of Paul's declaration, "Therefore, if any one is in Christ, he is a new creation; the old has passed away, behold, the new has come." One indication of its truth is the fact that all of the lay testimonies or letters previously quoted in this book were made by persons who have been in a *koinonia* group. A rereading at this point of some of those statements would serve as an eloquent witness to the depth of *koinonia* shared by many in these groups. Let us give two additional witnesses.

The first witness is from a group of couples who at this writing had shared one year together. This group included a remarkable variety of people. The age range was from twenty-five to seventy-one. The occupations of the men included, among others, retired school principal, personnel manager of a large department store, automobile mechanic, doctor, and salesman. The educational backgrounds of the persons included many with college degrees, some with only high school training, and one person who for reasons of health never reached high school. Imagine collecting such a group for a bridge party! Yet, in a matter of a few months, the people in this group entered into *koinonia* of a life-changing character for many of them. Here is the witness from a member of that group:

The Bible Study Group may afford its members an unusual experience, one that is all too uncommon even among seeking and sincere church members. *This is the experience of fellowship in Christ.* It is the experience of few other gatherings, because in a personal way this group may be both God-centered and God-entered. I say "may" happen, because it may not be true for all Bible Study Groups, and certainly is not necessarily true for all students of the Bible. But I believe that such was the experience of our study group and I feel privileged and somehow divinely touched to have been a part of this group.

It will be clear that when this woman talks about "fellowship in Christ" she is talking about *koinonia*. By definition *koinonia* is fellowship in Christ.

For four years I studied the Bible in school and college, with no greater effect on me than the accumulation of impersonal knowledge in any other field. My years of Bible study in school had been followed by a Philosophy of Religion course which cut loose all previous moorings and set me quite adrift. I felt I could not go to Church until I had honestly faced these questions and answered them in my own mind. I entered a Bible Study Group looking for a refresher course to follow up my previous study and hopefully to find the answers to some very basic religious questions.

Many students who study the Bible in college have this kind of disturbing experience. The question occurs as to the value of Bible courses in which childish bridges of faith are torn down, but where little is done to help build adult bridges. The church-related college clearly has a responsibility to provide Bible courses in which students are deliberately guided through the shoals of historical and literary criticism to the shore of an intellectually satisfying faith. This means fewer courses in which the Bible is studied as "great living literature," and more courses in which the Bible is unapologetically approached as the document of faith for the Christian.

I had not frankly and earnestly, or even casually, discussed religion with anyone for several years. Yet I found my initial reticence slowly disappearing in a gathering where everyone else had questions which they were willing to admit and for which they are sincerely trying to find the answers. I was impressed that there were others, persons I could respect, who cared about their religion, who were willing to share what they knew and as willing to admit what they did not know. Seeing how these people felt God had touched their lives and was still working in them, I began to see where I had also been touched and where God was working right now. I began to see that not all of my questions would be or even could be answered, but that I could live without the answers. I felt I had seen through a glass darkly and was now beginning to see face to face. The words of the Bible began to have pertinence as never before, to become contemporary instead of distant. It became apparent that the experience of God had been true for other lay people and could be true in my life. An overwhelming and awesome thought.

This woman made the great discovery that one can finally struggle through his doubts to a wholehearted and total trust in God, even though he knows there will remain problems and questions he may never fully understand or answer. She made this discovery in corporate study of the Bible, and found in the very human writings of the biblical books the living presence of the God about whom the books were written. The written Word became a vehicle for the Living Word in the context of *koinonia*.

Of our group my husband and I were probably the most critical in our approach to the Bible. If I therefore gained some insight that I had not even sought, I feel certain that others in the group also had their eyes opened, even if not in the same way. And the fact that we discovered this together in this group gave us a bond which we may call a fellowship, a fellowship in Christ. Perhaps a group could be formed with the specific purpose of becoming a fellowship in Christ, but to me it was the greater revelation for being so unexpected. It is perhaps better to gather a small group together to study the Bible, whatever their reasons for undertaking the study.

The experience of "fellowship in Christ" came as an unexpected dividend of meeting for Bible study. The sharing of *koinonia* was the by-product of a mutual concern. God surprised the people in the group with His presence, opening their eyes differently according to their different needs. This is the glorious economy of the Holy Spirit, whose varied grace is known in the context of Bible study.

A significant note is that three couples in that group have moved away from Cleveland, including the writer of this statement. If they were to be reached, it had to be *in one year*. This is a reminder that we must learn how to reach persons both quickly and deeply if their "conversions" are to endure.

The second witness comes from another group, the personnel of which included a young couple new to the church. Intelligent, well educated, exceedingly honest about their lack of Christian conviction, this man and woman began an earnest and sustained search for God. The year and a half which they shared in that group was a time of profound and permanent growth into Christ, a time of conversion. When this couple moved away from Cleveland, I wrote them asking that one of them set down some of the factors in their "conversion." The return letter speaks so clearly and honestly of their own experience, and the experience of many others in these groups, that I will quote from it extensively, with my own comments interspersed. As you read, note the writer's awareness of the church's loss of mission, the discovery of the need for real change, and the nature of this transforming change.

When you ask me to write something about my "conversion" in the past few years, it startles me because I always think of conversion as something that happens to someone else. Also I wonder if in writing about it I might fail to express what a possible sort of experience this can be. In reading about others, especially the more spectacular, I have felt that they were a different type, with an unusual pious bent quite different from me and my friends. But now I am convinced that the grace of God is available to anyone who seeks it.

Most church people believe that conversion is a rare and very emotional experience which surely is not intended for them. They do not believe that any radical changes are necessary in their lives; and church leaders have taught them not to expect any such changes.

I am sure that my religious background is similar to thousands of others brought up in a typical middle-class background. My family belonged to a Church much as one would belong to a club. That doesn't mean that they didn't devote a lot of time and work to its concerns, but it was an activity, not a Way of Life.

The church is an "activity" and not a "Way of Life" for most of our people. We have taught them to be busy in the activities of churches, but failed to lead them into the new life in Christ which is meant to be the very being of the church.

In school religion was a subject for study. A teacher once told us that a background in Homer and the Bible was essential to the understanding of English classical literature. A background is a good way of describing it—not as important as the foreground, but a nice thing to know, nevertheless. In college I wrestled with the problem of reality and concluded, along with a good many of my friends, that God was a cosmic force—the prime mover—the super brain which ruled the largest star and the tiniest atom with the natural law and scientific formula. God became unknowable to the human mind. One could only accept Him on existential terms, i.e. He exists because we want Him to exist, and that never seemed good enough. Most of us became budding humanists convinced of the futility, even hypocrisy of worship, feeling that its moral teachings were all that was left to justify the existence of the Church. And after studying the effect of the superego on man's personality, burdening him with senseless guilt and harmful taboos, I felt that religion might even prevent a person from realizing his full potential. Finally, my major was History with special interest in the Renaissance and the Reformation. There my knowledge of the Church was of a rich, corrupt, venal institution, caught at probably the worst point in its colorful history.

Many of our people believe that God is no more than a cosmic force. At best this is deism, at worst it is simply a pathetic hope. Many of our most highly educated and thoughtful people simply cannot love God with their minds, because they have not been led to grapple as adults with the problems and questions which have come to them as adults. Clearly the conventional Sunday School cannot cope with this matter. New and different forms of adult study are imperative. The *koinonia* group is indicated.

So by the time I was twenty I had made up my mind to dismiss God, Jesus, and the Church and religion in general. And I had plenty of company. When I got married my husband did not share my disbelief, but he too had become dismayed by the lack of conviction and mission in the Church. Yet he insisted we attend Church and seek to find a clearer understanding of its place in our lives. Since we moved around a good bit, we "shopped" for Churches. Minister after minister called on us at his request. I became an expert at getting rid of them fast. I just didn't want to get involved.

Perceptive laymen sense that the church and, sometimes, her leaders have lost their sense of mission. They see this in the lack of urgency in preaching, preaching which doesn't call for a verdict but settles for prudent behavior. They see this in the way the church reduces their calling as laymen to the performance of "practical" duties of administration and finance.

Then we found Aldersgate. It was not a prepossessing Church. It was small and unattractive—a room with pictures of Jesus on the walls and limp curtains at the windows—a most uninspiring place. And this is where just what I was afraid was going to happen, happened. We got involved. For me it started with a sermon, a sermon on what is probably an ancient sermon theme, the subject of values. It became apparent that whether we realize it or not we have a God! It may not be the God of the Jews, it may be the god of success or motherhood or humanism or security or quite a few other things, but like it or not we have it and we devote our lives to it. Following this came a prayer which seemed to bring us all into the presence of a listening God. It made one long to believe that God did exist and could be so concerned with us. This was no great turning point, but for the first time in a good while, I was forced to re-examine my philosophy.

This "awakening" took place in a service of worship. We will expect that God would awaken some of our people in the context of corporate worship. Our preaching and our praying and our conducting of a service of worship will thus be expectant and joyful, for we know that we meet in the presence of One who is transforming some of us. The new creation is taking place in our midst.

Re-examine, question, and then finding it hard work, try to forget the whole thing. This was the next stage. And with most Churches the whole thing would have died there. But Aldersgate had a dedicated group of people who would not let you alone. I was deluged

with books and understanding advice as I grew into spiritual ado-
lescence. This began what I can only describe as my own personal
experience with the Holy Spirit. I don't think this quite jibes with
the book definition, but what else can you call this troubling or deep
dissatisfaction close to physical anguish at not having an answer to
my questions. I feel that I have to seek whether I want to or not. I
have come to identify this feeling with that of the man who cried to
Jesus, "I believe, help Thou my unbelief!" It is more than a vague
insecurity, it is a persistent undeviating demand, and it is still with
me.

Decision leads to growth, to the struggle in which one is found
by God and thus finds himself. Here is described the relentless,
loving pursuit of the God who will not let us go, from whom we
can make no escape, who reaches out to find the lost sheep. In
this period of growth, the individual needs the encouragement
and sustaining friendship of those who understand because they
too have known the pains of growth and the struggle to believe.
This is a crucial time for the individual, because God is digging
deep into his inner being to lay the foundations for a mature
faith which cannot be shaken again.

A conversion is a turning about. For me it hasn't been so much
one identifiable experience as a process. It has been a growing and
developing arising out of a new relationship—an acute awareness of
the continual presence of God in my life. This happens not just in
moments of prayer, but all the time. The 139th Psalm puts it very
well; and all of us have the advantage of knowing the Christian God
who is loving, redemptive, and forgiving as well as omniscient, omnipotent, and omnipresent. I now know that He is an other-ness and
not just a reflection of me-ness. I know that I am never alone and
my concerns are His concerns. I know that He hears my prayers and
His hand is on my life.

This person describes what it means to know God. She expresses and relates firsthand knowledge of God. Most of our
church people do not have this firsthand experience. They are trying to live on the faith of their fathers and mothers. This is why
they do not know the power of the Holy Spirit, nor find the peace
and joy promised by Christ. Such people cannot be effective witnesses, for we can only witness to that which we ourselves know

firsthand. The purpose of the *koinonia* group is to lead people into this personal knowledge of God.

If I had to answer one of those signs one sees on the highway, "Are you saved?" I would have to say no. For I don't have the feeling of a *fait accompli*, I am not changed, I am changing. God is constantly making me aware that this is a long pull and that I am not in good condition. I need every bit of help I can get. Luckily there are some things that are a very positive help in following and understanding the Christian Way.

Here is conversion of a mature character. This person knows that she has not arrived spiritually; she is anything but pharisaical in her acknowledgment that she needs help. She goes ahead next to list some of the disciplines which proved to be of help to her.

Prayer. Prayer is a most important part of knowing God. He doesn't speak to us through fire or cloud or burning bush or even dreams, He speaks to us through prayer. To know someone well, one doesn't just find out about him academically, one seeks to know him personally. This is what prayer has become for me—knowing God personally. This hasn't been easy. My first prayers were shot through with an awareness that I might be talking to myself. At times I felt ridiculous in taking time from my clamoring family to get down on my knees before what could be a figment of the imagination. But self-delusion or not, this period became an important one. At last I had found a way to express thanks for all that I had received. At last through confession I rid myself of a few "chips" on my shoulder and dared to look at myself in the embarrassing light of revelation. At last I began to realize why there *must* be a redeeming Christ in the world to soften the judgment of a perfect God. I think most of us by attempting to justify ourselves, fall in the habits of self-deceit, rationalization, and self-forgiveness. Because we find ourselves unacceptable as we are, we try to think we are something we are not. In losing self-assurance, we become more sure of God.

Bible study. In addition to strength I received through prayer were challenging ideas in some well-written laymen's books plus of course the Bible. Studying on a solo basis didn't come easy—either you could pretend you understand and breeze through or else honestly stumble over each sentence. I tried both approaches and was mercifully saved by the formation of a Bible Study Group.

A Bible Study Group provides for a beginner some of the things he needs the most. In addition to a regular schedule of study, a climate of free exchange is established. There is great value in sharing experiences with others and seeing how they interpret Christianity in their lives; I also respected the keenness of insight and genuineness of growth among the members of our group. There is nothing quite so impressive or inspiring as watching a neighbor voice and answer questions ever so much better and with ever so much more understanding than you could. A group which lives this closely together inevitably becomes close-knit, *a training ground in miniature in Christian fellowship.*

Here is expressed the importance of the *koinonia* group in the early stages of conversion. This group is what the church is meant to be: "a training ground in miniature in Christian fellowship." Here many people "witness" and hear others "witness" for the first time. They are being prepared for their mission of witnessing in the world. In churches of several hundred members, Christian fellowship can be known by most people only in some small group.

Christian Fellowship. For Christian fellowship isn't a very real thing in these days of the big congregation. It is best felt in small groups such as a Bible Study Group or a prayer group or the choir. Isn't it too bad there aren't enough groups of this nature to cover everybody in the congregation? For instance I feel one of the best ways to feel part of a Church and to receive its special spirit is to join the choir. There is a regular meeting of members. It is small enough so you soon know everybody. It is a team effort with a tangible goal—not just busy work. The members have a chance to take an active part in the worship service. Through the blending of scripture and melody, the religious experience can be deepened—especially in works like Bach's *St. Matthew Passion* or the *Seven Last Words of Christ* or the *Messiah* or, really, many others. Many a non-musical member of the congregation may quarrel with this point of view, but though sometimes dissonant or off-key, the choir plays an important part in the lives of its own members. A Bible Study Group with good leadership can do the same thing, so could a teacher's seminar, or any group which is convened with a vital purpose rather than just for that catch-all word: Christian fellowship. In the Church to which I now belong there is a Women's Fellowship divided up in the Rug-Hooking group, the Mother's Club, and the Ladies Sewing Circle. My more outspoken friends refer to these as "stitch-and-bitch" clubs. This seems a pretty far cry from what Christian fellowship could be.

Many small groups within the existing structure of the life of the church could become *koinonia* groups. The choir, circles, committees, and youth groups are among these. It behooves the local church to transform those groups which can be transformed into *koinonia* groups. This is to emphasize the fact that *koinonia* is meant to be and can be known in many areas of the church's life which are currently closed to the Holy Spirit. The fact is we don't really expect people to be converted in the choir, or at a circle meeting, or at a committee meeting.

Layman Participation. You see, laymen do want to be involved in what in my youth was considered the minister's job. How can one fully worship God if he doesn't enter actively in the Sunday service? How can one carry out his Christian concern for others if he doesn't know and visit the sick and lonely in his own church? How can one give an adequate Christian witness in his community and place of work, if he hasn't learned to do it before his own fellow Church members? If the layman cannot perform these jobs, he is being deprived of true Protestant Christian participation. That is why it alarms me when a Church elected to have a minister to preach, an assistant minister to evangelize and visit the sick, a professional head of the education department, a student to lead the youth groups, a paid quartet, and finally an outside organization brought in to run the financial drive. All that is missing is a professional congregation. For these reasons I feel the Aldersgate emphasis on layman participation is one of the most exciting and rewarding policies. If I have had any growth in grace, some measure is because God has reached me in these avenues.

This paragraph on "Layman Participation" speaks of the emergence of the lay ministry. This is so important that discussion of it must be delayed until the next chapter. But this recovery of mission, this taking up of one's ministry, is always the fruit of genuine *koinonia*. This desire to serve and witness is an expression of the reality of the new creation. *Koinonia* is always expulsive, driving one deep into the being of the Church, and then driving one out into the world to fulfill the mission of the Church. The whole "conversion event" related by this writer is at least partially the experience of scores of people in the *koinonia* groups.

So much by way of documenting the new creation as it is manifest in changing lives in the *koinonia* groups. Surprising confirmation of the same experience with Bible Study Groups has recently come from those who work in the slum sections of our large cities.

In addressing the Cleveland (Ohio) Ministerial Association on the "Nature and Mission of the Church," Donald Benedict, who was the head of the Inner City Protestant Parish in Cleveland, said:

> Our experience over the past years indicates that the most significant thing in the life of our churches has been the continuous and systematic use of the Bible in the context of the "house church." It is here that the real questions people have about the Scripture as it relates to their lives come out. It is within this context that you sense the new life of the church emerging. Here is a real source of renewal for the church.

Now let me mention some things we have learned about these groups.

1. *Don't deliberately structure groups* around similar interests, experiences, and age levels. I did this with one group, and it was so homogeneous that the members missed the enrichment of differing background and experience which other groups have shared. The most mutually enriching experience will come to people whose differences of age, background, and outlook are shared and understood in *koinonia*.

2. *Don't raise every question in the book.* A minister or layman leading such a group should beware of raising personal questions which may not currently disturb any other member of the group. In the beginning, I raised all the doubts and problems I had known in my own quest for understanding. In the process I undermined the faith of some people unnecessarily. Now, I deal with problems and questions as they arise naturally in the context of the Bible study.

3. *Don't lecture; lead a discussion.* In the beginning, I used to open every meeting with a lecture or statement of some duration. This stultifies spontaneous question and discussion and makes the group members passive and nonparticipative. Now, we start out each meeting with a provocative question arising out of the text studied for that meeting. We use various techniques to stimulate discussion. One is to break down for several minutes into small "buzz groups" of four or five people, then return to the full group to share judgments reached. Or one can start by asking everyone present to write down his own judgment on a particular question, then permissively sharing the ideas that have come. Or one can

simply raise the question, and let it be discussed in normal spontaneous fashion.

4. *Learn to share prayer.* For most people in a beginning group, to pray in private is a matter of some mystery and much frustration. To pray in the presence of other people is, or so it seems, out of the question. We struggled with this in our groups, having a time of spontaneous prayer at the very end of the meeting. It was sometimes helpful, sometimes not, seldom fully satisfying. Then we heard of a method of sharing prayer which a group of men in a prayer group, not in our church, had used. It has transformed the prayer sharing in our groups. It is simply this. Each person is given opportunity to offer a sentence prayer in turn. If one has no prayer to offer, he simply says when it is his turn, "Amen." This is his participation, and likewise the signal to the next person that it is his turn. This device allows opportunity to every person, but takes the pressure off as well. The result has been a deeply meaningful sharing for many people and a discovery that one can be both helped and helpful in the sharing of prayer. The sharing of prayer has come to be of great importance in the knowledge of *koinonia* in a group.

5. *Try shared lay leadership.* We have moved consistently in the direction of lay leadership in these groups. We have reached the point where four of our five groups are led entirely by laymen. When a new group is started now, a couple with previous *koinonia* group experience leads the group. Rapidly this veteran couple leads the new people into the sharing of leadership. Within a few months, leadership is shared by all of those who wish to share it. Those persons or couples who are most capable of taking leadership of this kind are given specific training before they undertake the leadership of a beginning group.

6. *Don't expect a group to continue forever.* The tenure of a group may vary considerably. One of ours lasted in original form only one year. Three have lasted more than two years. One is in its fourth year. People move away from the community; some persons lose interest; new persons may come into the group. Each group develops its own personality and must evolve according to its own leading by the Holy Spirit. The time comes for every group when its usefulness is at an end. It should then be stopped.

7. *Group discipline is useful.* At the very beginning a group

should agree to attend a specific number of meetings, five or six, to give this experiment a chance. There should also be agreement to prepare the lesson material. When the fellowship of a group has become real, further group discipline may be discussed. A particular discipline should be set only after much discussion and when everyone is either content with it or willing that some others in the group shall share it. Such a discipline might include: the practice of daily prayer; prayer for each member of the group by name during the interval between meetings; a common mission either within the church or in the world.

A group may wish to undertake the sixfold discipline suggested in Chapter VI. Most people find the practice of such discipline more meaningful and satisfying in fellowship with others than by themselves. Indeed, there are few who have the strength to persist in such discipline without the encouragement of others engaged in it.

8. *Not everyone will be helped in these groups.* It is important to realize at the beginning that no one approach can possibly meet every single person at the point of his need. The *koinonia* group will not satisfy everyone in the same degree. Some will begin it but drop out shortly for a variety of reasons. In our experience, the overwhelming majority of those who have entered into it have found it deeply rewarding. Some have found it the most significant, life-changing experience in their lives.

9. *How to get one started in your church.* If at all possible, such a group should be started with the co-operation and guidance of the minister. He will know persons who have given indication of wanting to deepen their Christian faith and life. He can naturally and easily start such a group within the church's life. A series of teachers' meetings, a series of meetings during Advent or Lent, an announced seminar of stated duration—all these would serve as ways of introducing persons to *koinonia*. Such introductions will cause many persons to want more of the same.

A retreat is an excellent way to bring people to consideration of such a group. One winter, twenty-two of our men spent a two-day weekend on a retreat. Many of the men were awakened to decisions—some to start regular daily prayer, some to read the Bible, some to try telling the *whole* truth in business dealings. Some became concerned to start a prayer group. In fact, three men's prayer groups were started and sustained, partly from the impact of that retreat. A *koinonia* group could emerge from the impetus of such a retreat, and, indeed, one man was inspired to start a new *koinonia* group.

A similar retreat was held a few months later for twenty-one women of our church. Again, many came back determined to continue that to which they had been awakened on the retreat. A second women's prayer group resulted.

A concerned layman or couple could start such a group simply by inviting two or three other couples in for an evening and proposing that they meet for a stated number of evenings to study a Gospel together. The young woman whose conversion experience was related earlier in this chapter believes that the Bible Study Group is an experience which should be shared when at all possible by a man and wife together. She writes:

I would seriously question the validity of a faith we couldn't both share. Maybe this is feminine weakness, but I feel that women are inclined to get off on emotional binges or follow certain fads. If something appeals to women only I suspect it. If it is something worthwhile, it is worthwhile for both of us. And if I have any advice to offer a beginning Bible Study Group, it is to encourage couples to join.

This is good advice. In our experience, couples have formed the nucleus of every group. Having the groups meet in the evening makes it possible for men to share in it. The home becomes the place and setting for *koinonia*. The least effective group we have had was a group in which there were many "singles" (husband without wife, or wife without husband) and few couples. In addition, an experience as potentially meaningful as the Bible Study Group ought to be shared by a couple together, whenever possible. This allows them to grow together, to share on a deeper level than ever before. Many couples are enabled to talk together about their faith for the first time.

One of the most effective ways of starting a new group is in the training of persons for membership in the church. Since this is so important and since it is a remarkable vehicle for lay ministry within the church, considerable space will be given to the subject in the next chapter. These, then, are some general comments arising from our experience with the *koinonia* groups.

A final word on the personal value of these groups for a minister. These groups keep me from being in spiritual isolation. They enable me to share in the new creation. In times of dryness or despair or just plain weariness, when I would rather go home, I go to one of these meetings. Someone in the time of quiet offers a prayer, and I am ministered to. Someone shares an insight or an experience; I watch the light of dawning faith break forth on someone's face; I look at these couples who have hired baby-sitters in order to come and seek God together—and I am lifted up. I watch the Holy Spirit working in their lives, and I am warmed and encouraged. I have a box seat for the constantly new and exciting drama of changed and changing lives. There is nothing more joyful than beholding people who are being transformed. To be at the growing edge of another's conversion is to share the joy in heaven over one sinner who repents.

I have discovered I am now dependent on this *koinonia*, this holy fellowship. If I were to go to another church, the first thing I would do is try to create such a group, for my own selfish need. These groups keep me closer to the people. They serve to sharpen and in some instances modify my own judgments and interpretations. I have learned more from the people in these groups than from many books about the new life in Christ. Often I have gone, like John Wesley, "unwillingly" to a *koinonia* group meeting and have come away with my own heart-warming experience in which God refreshed and powered me to go on.

There is implied here a very real sharing of the new creation by clergymen and lay people together. Paul speaks of his "laymen" as partners in the gospel, "partakers with me of grace . . . true yokefellow . . . fellow workers" (Philippians 1:7; 4:3). Paul speaks as though he and they are engaged in the same mission. In the last chapter of this book we shall examine the role of the clergyman as he fulfills *his* ministry in preparing his lay people for *their* ministry. The church becomes in truth the new creation of God as laymen take up their ministry. The most significant outcome of the *koinonia* groups is the emerging new order of lay ministry.

XI

New Creation in the Church:
The Lay Ministry Emerges

And his gifts were . . . for the equipment of the
saints, for the work of ministry. . . .

EPHESIANS 4:11–12

The mission of the church is the conversion of the world. We
are called to go and make disciples of all nations, to be witnesses
where we are and to the end of the earth. Our problem is that
we have usually sent boys to do a man's job. We have sent un-
converted people to convert others. We exhort our people to win
others to Christ, when they themselves have not been won. The
modern church has been high on the techniques of evangelism
but low on personal knowledge of the God who sends us into the
world. The church exists for the sake of the world, but before the
world can be redeemed, the church must become the Body of
Christ. Only the Body of Christ can be salt, light, and leaven in
the world. The Christian exists for the sake of his non-Christian
world, but before he can be of saving help to that world he must
become a disciple of Christ himself. Only a *disciple of Christ* can
become an *apostle for Christ*.

The *koinonia* groups provide the context in which the institutional church may begin to become the Body of Christ, and in
which nominal church members may become disciples of Christ.
Within such groups Christians are being equipped for the work
of ministry, first in the church and then in the world. From such
groups the lay ministers are coming. Genuine disciples of Christ
inevitably want to take up their ministry. They do not have to
be exhorted; they only need guidance and opportunity. They
recognize and acknowledge that they have been "created in Christ

Jesus for good works" (Ephesians 2:10). They desire to serve and witness. Let me requote here the pertinent statement of the woman whose conversion is cited in the previous chapter:

You see, laymen do want to be involved in what in my youth was considered the minister's job. How can one fully worship God if he doesn't enter actively in the Sunday service? How can one carry out his Christian concern for others if he doesn't know and visit the sick and lonely in his own church? How can one give an adequate Christian witness in his community and place of work, if he hasn't learned to do it before his own fellow church members? If the layman cannot perform these jobs, he is being deprived of true Protestant Christian participation.

That statement might be amended to begin: "Laymen who are being converted do want to be involved, etc." for the willing acceptance of ministry is not visible in the average church member. In fact, one mark of the new creation is precisely this desire to share in the ministry. This is conscious discipleship; it is the priesthood of all believers. It is the true *koinonia*, the participation in the Body of Christ. We are watching the emergence of the lay ministry.

It is difficult to give any precise description of the ways in which the lay ministry appears and comes into being in the church. We can't really stop the moving picture for purpose of analysis. It is still too early to assess what is happening. We can never tabulate the workings of the Holy Spirit. Nevertheless, it is possible to make some observations on the emerging lay ministry.

First, *the lay ministers are becoming leaders in the church.* A list of the positions held by persons who have been in *koinonia* groups in our church would include:

Chairman of the Board of Trustees
Chairman of the Commission on Finance*
Chairman of the Commission on Education*
Chairman of the Commission on Evangelism*
Chairman of the Commission on the Mission of the Church*
Superintendent and Assistant Superintendent of the Sunday School
Sunday School teacher (two-thirds of the teacher group)
President of the Men's Fellowship

*These happen to be the four major areas of the work of the Methodist Church as outlined in the Methodist Discipline.

President of the Woman's Society of Christian Service
Official Board member (one-half of the Board members)
Layman who trains new members (nearly all such laymen)

Someone asked me how this transfer of leadership to so many people in these groups could legitimately occur in a local church. The answer is fourfold. We have a system of rotation which allows at most three-year tenure for important positions of leadership. The laymen in the *koinonia* groups are able and willing to serve. Others recognize their genuine concern and respect it. I, as the minister, have had opportunity through the fellowship of the groups to know group members better than I know most other church members. Therefore, I naturally think of persons in *koinonia* groups when need for leadership arises.

The crucial nerve centers of our church are increasingly being manned by people who have lived in the conditions for *koinonia*. This means that they have had opportunity to learn of the nature and purpose of the church. They have shared fellowship in Christ. They have been trained, as it were, to be spiritual leaders. There is greater hope that such persons will have the vision and courage under God to engage upon the mission of the church. There is the possibility that we shall recover our mission to the world.

Second, *the lay ministers are operating as leaven in the church*. It puzzled me at first to watch some people who had not been in the *koinonia* groups take up their ministry as effectively and powerfully as those who had been in the groups. It finally struck me that the *koinonia* groups have been serving unconsciously as leaven in the church. Persons in these groups begin to witness, and they infect others. The climate in the church has become favorable to personal witness. The whole idea of the lay ministry is acceptable now, where it was unknown before. People who are growing in other ways than in the context of the *koinonia* groups are now invited to share their growth, to take up their ministry. The influence of the people in the *koinonia* groups is truly like leaven—often hidden, usually quiet and gradual, but permeating the total membership. So the company of lay ministers is far larger than simply the number of persons who have been in *koinonia* groups. For the last two years, 10 per cent of the active membership of the church has been involved in these groups. Over a period of five years approximately one hundred fifty people have been in the groups. It is impossible to calculate the impact and influence these persons have exercised in the life of the church. But it is clear that they have made the lay ministry a live and appealing possibility for all concerned church members.

Third, *the lay ministers are accepting the call to preach.* When I am gone on a Sunday morning, the chances are good that one of our laymen will preach. In the last three years, twenty of our own laymen have preached on Sunday morning. During the last calendar year, eight laymen preached. About three-fourths of the preachers have been men; and one-fourth, women. Our laymen preach the Sundays when I am on vacation in the summer. Their sermons are usually in the nature of personal witness. Let me quote statements from two such sermons. The first was preached by a man at the beginning of his awakening and growth toward maturity in Christ. He expresses the questions of one who is becoming a disciple of Christ:

Let me say first that I am not here to preach a sermon. My purpose today is to share with you some *questions* I have. They are questions which many Protestant laymen probably have or should have. I don't propose to answer them, principally because I don't think I can. But I would like for you to share my concern.

Have we in the church deluded ourselves into believing that we are serving God to the fullest when we are only promoting neighborliness and good citizenship? Is there too much "togetherness" and not enough "with God-ness"?

In order for the church to be everything to everybody, are we watering down the authority and doctrine and the principles of the church? Maybe I'm getting into deep water; maybe I don't know what I'm talking about, but I do know that the easiest thing in the world to do is to become and stay a member in good standing of a Protestant Church in suburbia.

In short, is salvation—which I believe is the ultimate purpose of our Christian mission—really as easy as we make it? Believe me, I wish it were, but frankly I'm frightened that it probably isn't.

One who is asking, seeking, and knocking in this fashion will grow. He will help others to grow because he will puncture their complacency, as his own has been punctured.

The second sermon was preached by a woman who is clearly well along the path of discipleship. In this sermon she reflects upon two years of growth in a *koinonia* group, and in the larger context of the church's life.

The first time I ever attended Aldersgate Church was almost two years ago, and coincidentally, on Layman's Sunday. I came to Church not looking for peace of mind or spiritual comfort or fellowship for myself—in my ignorance I was convinced I had these—but looking rather for a Sunday School for my children. There are probably many people who do that, who believe, as I did then, that a good Christian needn't himself go to Church, but he does at least owe to his children the nurturing of Christian character provided by the Sunday School.

I suppose, whether I realized it or not, I adhered to the humanist school of thought. I found that much of what I had read in the past seemed to stress the moralistic approach to religion, so common unfortunately, even in the pulpit today. Of course, the Bible was not exactly on my reading list. To me it was purely a collection of inspirational songs and sayings for anyone who had the time for this antiquated literature. However, I still considered myself a Christian because I led a reasonably good life and minded my own business.

Don and I became members a very short time after our first appearance here, possessing, I suppose, what we refer to as Christian character, but poorly educated in the real meaning of Christian discipleship.

About the time I joined the Church I began to wonder and to think. I wondered if what is called peace of mind isn't often just a dangerously disguised form of complacency. Is a Church or religion supposed to endow us at all, in fact, with the elusive peace of mind? Should we come to Church just so that we may leave feeling safe, satisfied, and secure in the knowledge that "God's in His Heaven, all's right with the world"? Here I began to be seriously disturbed— God may be in His Heaven, all right, but surely all was not right with the world—or with the country, or community, or with my own family, not even—especially not, with myself. Here was where I must begin. I needed to be changed. But how?

Gradually, through Bible study and prayer, I began to realize that it's not enough merely to lead a good life and possess this Christian character that is so often the final goal of our Sunday School teaching. I learned through studying the life and teachings of Jesus and reading Acts and some of Paul's letters that the original Christian Church was *not* a cult of moralism. We are sadly deluding ourselves if we think that because times have changed, our pace of life has quickened, our knowledge and training in science have increased, that we no longer need to rely on God, but consider ourselves so self-sufficient that we accept Jesus Christ merely as a guide to moral living. We cannot believe this and call ourselves Christians, no matter how good our lives or fine our characters are. We must go further and become genuine Christian disciples and learn with others as the early Christians did of the Christian Way. Then our relationship with God, through Christ, is not a separate one-day-a-week departure from our lives. As Christian disciples we learn that Christ is for us all, personally. We learn that we are not just "ordinary Christians," different from the clergy and a few other dedicated individuals; but that their responsibilities and obligations are our responsibilities and obligations. We are also the Church—even you and I. We are granted the privilege of possessing not just a warm glow of peace of mind, but the greater warmth of spiritual tranquility which is fellowship in Christ.

This woman describes a pilgrimage which is characteristic of many of our lay ministers. A number of young couples first look for a church out of concern that their children receive some religious education. Unconsciously perhaps, these people are Unitarians, thinking of Jesus exclusively as the great teacher. They confuse decent behavior with the new life in Christ, and suppose that their decent behavior means they are Christians. As such people come into *koinonia* groups, they discover that they need to be changed, that their idea of the Christian life is far less demanding and less exciting than the New Testament picture of this life. They discover that they are meant to be ministers of Christ, like the lay people described in the New Testament. When a layman speaks of his own pilgrimage before the congregation, the people listen and take heed as they seldom do when a professional clergyman says the same things.

It is important for the people of a church to discover that some of their own number are earnestly trying to live as disciples of Christ. Occasional lay preaching on Sunday morning is an excellent means to this end. But more, it is important that we recognize the layman's call to preach. We are being reminded that the pulpit is not the private precinct of the clergy but the sacred function of that ministry in which both clergy and laymen share. As some clergymen are *not* called to preach, some lay ministers are called to preach. Occasional lay preaching on a Sunday morning allows those lay ministers who have the gift of preaching to give their gift to the church.

Fourth, *the lay ministers are training others for their ministry.*

The lay ministers are now undertaking the teaching function which has usually been reserved for the clergyman. They are the organizers and leaders of prayer groups. They take leadership in the *koinonia* groups. They undertake the training of young people for membership in the church. They witness to parents who meet for instruction before their children are to be baptized. At such meetings, we speak of the history and meaning of the sacrament of Baptism in the church. One layman speaks of the necessity of growth ourselves in order that we become able to help our children grow in faith. He describes the *koinonia* groups as the most promising context for growth. Another layman describes how he and his wife share prayer together, and indicates that a husband and wife who are praying together will naturally include their children in such family prayer when the time comes. The hope of this lay witness is that some parents will be awakened to their own need for growth in the Christian life. For some people, the sacrament of Baptism becomes the means of grace it is intended to be for all people.

Perhaps the most significant development in the emergence of the lay ministry has occurred in the training of adult new members. Within the last year we have been enabled to create the conditions for *koinonia* for prospective new members. The witness of our lay ministers has been the key factor. Here is what has happened.

From the very beginning of my ministry, I was concerned at the obvious meaninglessness of church membership for large numbers of church members. I could see that my church, like most others, was crowded with nominal members, scarcely aware of the new life in Christ which the New Testament offers to, and demands of, all disciples of Christ. And it was clear that our customary procedure of adding new members without the slightest bit of real challenge to commitment in New Testament dimension was at the core of the problem. I believed that somehow we needed to train and prepare people for meaningful membership in the church.

I could not forget Jesus' words on the conditions of discipleship as they appear in the eighth, ninth, and tenth chapters of the Gospel according to Mark. Jesus was challenging His followers to total, unconditional commitment to Himself, saying clearly that if a man were not ready for such commitment, He had no use for him. I could not forget Jesus' final words to His followers after His resurrection, as recorded by Matthew, "Go and make disciples"—not build up the church rolls, not sweep in the neighborhood, not get church members, but *go and make disciples!* And I knew that many good, attractive people coming into the church had not the vaguest conception of this "discipleship" Jesus was talking about. *And it was our fault!* We of the church had made no attempt to make it clear. This we must do. Our first plan was to arrange meetings for all prospective new members.

We asked all persons seeking membership in Aldersgate Church to come to preparatory meetings, whatever church background they had or did not have, because we knew that membership in a church of any denomination was no guarantee that one was a growing, committed disciple of Christ. In fact, in experience we have learned that among the people seeking membership in the church, there are always three groups. The largest group consists of nominal Christians; the next in size is the group of happy, genial pagans; and the smallest group is always the group of committed, growing disciples of Christ. We have learned that everyone needs the awakening power of the Holy Spirit, for whose work we try to provide the conditions in these new-member meetings.

At first we had a series of three meetings, in lecturer-listener style. Laymen were involved at the beginning, and before long most of the training was being done by them. The meetings were valuable, and to some very meaningful, but somehow we hadn't yet found the key to open hearts and minds as we knew we must.

Then we tried a different approach. We decided to have six meetings. A major change was the spending of at least half of each meeting in small groups, separating men and women. These groups were led by laymen, and provided a context in which person-to-person encounter could facilitate real discussion of the areas of Christian discipleship. And suddenly, the Holy Spirit was there, awakening people, stirring them, disturbing them, causing many to begin asking, seeking, and knocking as never before. Suddenly we found that we were sharing *koinonia*, that fellowship in Christ, that fellowship of the Spirit which is the unique gift of the church to the world. The results in terms of lives changed and changing were thrilling. We are still experimenting and making changes, both in procedure and material used. We have already taken four groups of people through these meetings. Our practice is described below, although doubtless some changes will occur as time passes.

We have come to understand our purpose in these meetings to be the providing of conditions in which the Holy Spirit will awaken people to commit themselves to Christ, to start growing, and then to give them specific help on how to continue growing in Christ. Far and away the most effective means of doing this has been the witness of laymen, the sharing of personal faith in the context of *koinonia*, the *koinonia* which many know for the first time in the small discussion groups in the new-member meetings. Here is an outline of the six meetings:

FIRST MEETING

I.   *Opening lecture by minister*   (THIRTY MINUTES)

A.   Welcome to new people
B.   Procedure of meetings:
    1. Opening talks
    2. Discussion groups: small groups of six to eight persons; role of lay leaders
    3. Concluding talks
    4. Refreshments and fellowship
C.   Résumé of topics to be covered in the six meetings
D.   Purpose of meetings: challenge people to commit or recommit themselves to Christ
    1. Make clear that church membership should be the outer expression of Christian discipleship
    2. Present picture of nominal church membership characteristic of our time
    3. Contrast this with the exciting discipleship of the early Christians, as portrayed in Acts
    4. State that these meetings are an attempt to do something about this contrast

II.   *Discussion groups*   (ONE HOUR)

A.   Opening conversation
    1. Lay leaders introduce themselves

      2. New people introduce themselves
B. Leaders raise one or more of these questions:
      1. What has church membership meant to you in the past?
      2. What are you looking for in this church?
      3. Do you think it is necessary to be affiliated with a church in order to be a "good Christian"?
        (People answer verbally or write answers which are then read by leader and discussed)
C. Leaders witness to their own pilgrimage of faith
      1. Superficiality of their own church membership for many years
      2. Events in which they awakened to the new life of discipleship
D. Intended result of discussion: new people examine their own motives in seeking membership, and begin to grasp the exciting possibility of the life of discipleship

III. *Concluding remarks by minister*   (FIFTEEN MINUTES)

A. Many will begin to find the new life in Christ
B. Further meetings will indicate why and how the new life comes in Christ
C. Be ready for adventure and risk, for in Christ one's life is no longer his own
D. Reading assignment for next meeting:
      1. Bible (persons are urged to secure a Revised Standard Version)
        a. Luke 22: Peter's denial of Christ
        b. Acts 2–5: Peter as the dynamic leader of the early church
        c. Question: What happened to change Peter?
        d. Answer: Read Luke 23, 24
      2. *The Significance of the Church:* chapters I, III, IV[1]

IV. *Refreshments and fellowship*

SECOND MEETING

I. *Opening lecture by minister*   (THIRTY MINUTES)

A. The risen Christ changed Peter
      1. Peter before the crucifixion (Luke 22)
      2. Peter after the resurrection (Acts 2–5)
      3. Peter's conversion through the impact of the death and resurrection of Christ
B. The risen Christ has changed many in His church
      1. Paul

      2. Martin Luther
      3. John Wesley
C. The risen Christ is changing lives among us
      1. Fact of conversion to new life of some persons in our church
      2. Questions:
         a. What is the nature of this new life in Christ?
         b. How does it differ from the old life?
         c. How does one enter the new life?

II. *Discussion groups* (ONE HOUR)

A. Leaders describe characteristics of the old and new life
      1. The old life:
         a. Man the central figure
         b. Pride, self-sufficiency, pursuit of one's own happiness
         c. Guilt, anxiety, lack of meaning in life
         d. Refusal to acknowledge need of others or of God
      2. The new life in Christ:
         a. God becoming the central figure
         b. Awareness of one's limitations—dawning humility
         c. Experience of forgiveness—inner tranquillity, joy
         d. Growing compassion for sufferings of others
         e. Rising urgency to discover and fulfill one's mission
         f. Dependence upon Christian fellowship
B. Leaders witness concerning their own experience of:
      1. The old and new life
      2. Their current struggles
      3. Search
      4. Discoveries
C. Leaders raise questions:
      1. Do you know anyone whom Christ is changing?
      2. Have you any experience of the new life yourself?
D. Intended result of discussion: new people see that the new life is possible for the ordinary layman, and are encouraged to look for it in Christ's church

III. *Concluding remarks by minister* (FIFTEEN MINUTES)

A. Christ is the new life
      1. He confronts us in His body, the church
      2. He comes to us in *koinonia*
B. We receive Him in faith
      1. Trust

    2. Commitment—the leap of faith

    3. Obedience—the life of discipleship

C. The experience of the new life:

    1. Awakening to decision for Christ

    2. Growth to maturity in Christ

    3. The disciplines of discipleship

D. Reading assignment for next meeting:

    1. Bible

       a. John 3:1–8

       b. II Corinthians 5:16–20

    2. *The Experiment of Faith:* chapters I, II[2]

IV.   *Refreshments and fellowship*

THIRD MEETING

I.   *Opening lecture by minister*   (THIRTY MINUTES)

A. The six aspects of discipleship

    1. Worship

    2. Prayer

    3. Bible study

    4. Service

    5. Giving

    6. Witness

B. Worship

    1. Why we worship: obey God's command to do so

    2. What worship is: offering ourselves to God

    3. How we worship:

       a. Isaiah 6:1–8 provides theological pattern for our particular order of worship

       b. Give each person a copy of a typical Sunday morning bulletin

       c. Explain our order of worship with reference to the movements of adoration, confession, affirmation of faith, and consecration

C. The meaning of the sacraments:

    1. Baptism

    2. Holy Communion

D. Explain meaning of the symbols in our sanctuary and also the meaning of symbolic actions which take place during service

II.   *Discussion groups—prayer*   (ONE HOUR)

A. Leaders ask question: Why do you or don't you pray?
1. Discussion should bring forth the common barriers to prayer and the meaning found in prayer by those present
B. While leading discussion on these matters, leaders will witness at appropriate times to the meaning of prayer in their own lives:
1. Why we pray: to know personal, direct fellowship with God
2. What is prayer: personal fellowship with God
a. The five fingers of prayer: adoration, confession, thanksgiving, petition, intercession
b. Varieties of prayer: "flash" prayers, meditation, specific period of time set aside for prayer
3. How, when, where to pray:
a. Leaders in women's groups give specific suggestions for daily prayer discipline suitable to home situation
b. Leaders in men's groups give specific suggestions for daily prayer discipline suitable for various work situations
4. Family prayers:
a. Husband and wife
b. Parents and children
5. Prayer groups in the life of the church
C. Give to each person a copy of the *Upper Room* or similar devotional guide
D. Intended result of discussion: new people challenged to begin a meaningful discipline of daily prayer

III.   *Concluding remarks by minister*   (FIFTEEN MINUTES)

A. Regular worship central for growing disciples of Christ
B. Urge people to make earnest experiment in daily prayer
C. Reading assignment for next meeting:
1. Bible:
a. Prayers in the Psalms: Psalms 51, 103, 139, etc.
b. Prayers in the New Testament: John 17, Ephesians 3:14–21, Philippians 1:3–11
2. Pamphlet: *Teach Us To Pray*[3]
3. *The Significance of the Church:* chapter VI

IV.   *Refreshments and fellowship*

FOURTH MEETING

I.   *Opening lecture by minister*   (TWENTY MINUTES)

A. The vocation of ministry: refer to Mark 10:42–45 and Matthew 25:31–46
B. The ministry of the clergy: equip the people for their ministry
   1. Make clear the minister is available at any time for personal help
   2. State personal habits of study, calling, etc.
C. The lay ministry: refer to I Corinthians 12 and Ephesians 4
   1. The calling to serve
   2. The calling to give
   3. The calling to witness

II.   *Discussion groups—service*   (ONE HOUR)

A. Leaders discuss the meaning of service as the active fulfillment of Jesus' command to love God and neighbor
B. Leaders in men's groups lead discussion on service:
   1. At work:
      a. Doing the best one can in his job
      b. Loving neighbor and even enemy in his job
   2. At home:
      a. Service to one's wife
      b. Service to one's children
      c. Service around the house
   3. In the church
   4. In the community
C. Leaders in women's groups lead discussion on service:
   1. At home:
      a. Service to one's husband
      b. Service to one's children
      c. Housework
   2. In the neighborhood
   3. In the church
   4. In the community
D. Intended result of discussion: new people begin to view all of daily life as the realm of personal, loving service to others, and make fair distribution of time and energy to service in the family, in the church, and in the community
E. Leaders give to each person an information sheet listing ways of service within the life and mission of the church; the sheets are filled out at home and handed in at next meeting

III.   *Panel discussion on Bible study*   (TWENTY-FIVE MINUTES)

A. Minister gives brief history of Bible Study Groups in the church

B. Couples witness to their experiences in Bible Study Groups:
    1. Procedure at a typical meeting
    2. Chance for firsthand knowledge of the Bible
    3. Sharing one's doubts, beliefs, experiences with others
    4. Husband and wife share spiritual growth together
    5. Best way of exposing oneself to the transforming work of the Holy Spirit
    6. Urge new people to join group being started soon

IV.　Reading assignment for next meeting:

A. Bible
    1. Mark 10
    2. Matthew 25
    3. John 13
    4. I Corinthians 12
    5. Ephesians 4
B. *The Experiment of Faith:* chapters III, V

V.　Refreshments and fellowship

FIFTH MEETING

I.　Opening lecture by Finance Chairman of the local church
(TWENTY-FIVE MINUTES)

A. Biblical foundations of giving:
    1. Old Testament tithe
    2. New Testament:
        a. Attitude of Jesus: Matthew 6:19–34; Mark 10:17–31
        b. Loving liability in early church: Acts 2, 4
        c. Proportional giving: I Corinthians 16; II Corinthians 9
B. A contemporary view of tithing
    1. Ten per cent of income after taxes
    2. This 10 per cent distributed to church, charities, etc.
    3. Tithing experience among our church members
C. The financial structure and operation of the church
    1. Give to each person a copy of the annual budget
    2. Explain major items in budget, noting in detail that portion of the budget which supports the work of Christ beyond local church
    3. Pledging:

    a. Disciplined commitment for individual
    b. Enables church to project anticipated income

II.   *Discussion Groups—giving*   (THIRTY MINUTES)

A. Leaders humbly witness to their own awakening, growth, and struggle in the giving of money
B. Leaders solicit any further questions on budget and pledging
C. Leaders stress the obligation to pledge
    1. Pledge a discipline like daily prayer, Sunday worship, etc.
    2. Pledge card given to each person; card explained
    3. People asked to fill out card at home, bring it back to the sixth and last meeting
D. Intended result of discussion: new people will be moved to consider seriously a measure of sacrificial giving as a start toward tithing

III. *Brief history of the Christian church by layman or minister*
                                    (TWENTY-FIVE MINUTES)

A. New Testament growth and expansion
B. The formation of Roman Catholic and Orthodox communions
C. The Reformation and Protestantism
D. The Ecumenical Movement

IV. Sketch of denomination by layman   (Twenty-five minutes)

A. Origin and originators
B. History
C. Main doctrinal emphases
D. Polity

V. Reading assignment for next meeting:

A. Bible
    1. Mark 10
    2. Acts 2, 4
    3. II Corinthians 9
B. *The Significance of the Church*: chapters II, V
C. The denominational primer

VI. *Refreshments and fellowship*

SIXTH MEETING

I. Opening lecture on the local church by lay leader

(THIRTY MINUTES)

A. History
B. Polity
C. The life and mission of this church:
    1. Give to each person a copy of the Annual Report of the church
    2. Explain group life in the church
    3. Explain the various commissions and committees

II. Discussion groups—witness (ONE HOUR)

A. Leaders discuss the nature and purpose of Christian witness
    1. What witness is not: exhibitionist imposition
    2. What witness is: sharing the good news, sharing our faith in Christ
    3. Jesus' command: ". . . you shall be my witness . . ." (Acts 1:8)
B. Leaders raise questions for discussion:
    1. Has anyone ever witnessed to you?
    2. Have you had occasion to witness to anyone?
C. Leaders of men's groups lead discussion on witness:
    1. At work:
        a. Moral issues of current interest (race relations, juvenile delinquency, etc.) and their implications for persons committed to Christ
        b. Personal needs of those with whom one works
    2. At home: sharing faith with one's wife and children
    3. In the church
    4. In the community
D. Leaders of women's groups lead discussion on witness:
    1. At home:
        a. Sharing faith with one's husband
        b. Taking major responsibility for arranging family prayer
        c. Taking major responsibility for teaching children to pray
    2. In the neighborhood:
        a. Moral issues of current interest
        b. Personal needs of one's neighbors
    3. In the church
    4. In the community
E. Retreats discussed

F. Intended result of discussion: new people begin to view all of daily life as the realm of personal witness and make fair distribution of time and energy to witness in the family, church, and community

III.   *Concluding remarks and fellowship*   (THIRTY MINUTES)

A. Reading suggestion: finish reading material received
B. Give to each person an evaluation sheet, asking that later at home he write comments on the procedures, materials, and personal meaning of these six meetings and that he mail the sheet to the church within the next few days
C. Explain the vows in the membership reception ceremony
D. Explain the procedure of membership reception
E. Give to each person a copy of *My Commitment to Christian Discipleship* (see below), to be kept by each person as a reminder of the meaning of membership in the church
F. Receive pledge cards in offering plate
G. The sharing of Holy Communion
H. Benediction

MY COMMITMENT TO CHRISTIAN DISCIPLESHIP

I understand that becoming a member of a Christian Church is the external sign of my inner commitment of life to Jesus Christ. I further understand that there are specific actions which a growing committed Christian will undertake. These will include:

1. *Worship*
   Regular attendance upon public worship of God in my Church.
2. *Prayer*
   The daily practice of seeking God's guidance and power through prayer.
3. *Bible*
   The reading of the Bible on my own individual plan, or in fellowship with others in a Bible study or prayer group.
4. *Giving*
   The pledging of my financial support to the work of God's Church.
5. *Service*
   Offering myself to be used within the life of Church and community to live out Jesus' command, "Love your neighbor."
6. *Witness*
   Seeking opportunities to share my faith with others in my daily life and associations.

I accept this challenge to Christian Discipleship, and pledge my earnest intent to do these things, by the grace of God, and in fellowship with other Christian Disciples.

Signature_____

The results have convinced us that we are on the right track in these meetings. Following are statements on the evaluation sheets received from some of the new members:

I already feel closer to this church than to any other I have been associated with.

I will be eternally grateful for the privilege of being a part of this group.

This church and I came to know each other.

I came to feel that the church needs me almost as much as I need the church.

I was tremendously pleased to see the very sincere approach to these membership meetings. I have learned more about this church in four meetings than I've learned during my full association with other churches. The quality of leadership, the breadth of approach, and the depth of tolerance have become apparent from these meetings.

I was greatly impressed with the whole procedure, and just wish I could have had this years ago.

These meetings have served a great benefit to me in many ways, but most of all they have reminded me of the glory of prayer. Being inactive in church had caused me to become a lazy Christian, and these meetings have renewed my hunger for knowledge and service.

I like the idea that these classes are compulsory—gives more meaning to membership. [Actually, in extenuating circumstances, persons are not required to attend all the meetings.]

I wish we could continue these meetings right into our time of membership.

One man came up to me after the small-group discussion on "witness" and said:

Why, this is a revelation to me! These fellows [he was referring to the three laymen who conducted the group meeting on "witness"] are ordinary, good guys, and they talk as though their faith really *means* something to them. They are trying to *live* their faith in their work and trying to get it across to others. I feel that maybe my faith can become real to me like theirs.

This man had missed the first two meetings of prospective new members, being out of town as a salesman on the road. He told me he had finally consented to come to the third meeting, grumbling all the way. He was a nominal member of a church in the city from which he had moved to Cleveland. In this small discussion group he had an "awakening," whose results even he couldn't forecast at that time.

He took the book *The Experiment of Faith* with him on a business trip, and read it. A few days later I received a telephone call from him; he asked me to come over to talk with him. When I got there, he described how he had read the book and had come to a sentence in which the author cautioned the would-be Christian to make honest repentance for the sins of the past before venturing seriously on the life of discipleship. In a few moments of honest self-exposure and prayer, this man was released from the old life and launched into the new life in Christ. He and his wife began to have prayer together. They came into a *koinonia* group. He started teaching Sunday School. They literally entered upon a new life in Christ. Within three months he had won another couple to the church. And it all started when the Holy Spirit awakened him in that meeting of prospective new members.

A concrete result of the meetings we have held for four different groups of prospective new members is the fact that nearly half the persons in each group came into new *koinonia* groups. We are learning how to reach people both quickly and deeply. One couple in the first group of new members trained in this way came into a new *koinonia* group. Three months later they found themselves involved in the training of new people in the second new-member group.

Those who are new to the life of discipleship seem able to witness with freshness and gladness of heart to others on the verge of this life. We have come to understand a main purpose of these training meetings as awakening persons to join a *koinonia* group. Our experience confirms that of John Wesley, who wrote:

I was more convinced than ever that the preaching like an Apostle, without joining together those that are awakened, and training them up in the ways of God, is only begetting children for the murderer. How much preaching has there been for these twenty years all over Pembrokeshire! But no regular societies, no discipline, no order or connection; and the consequence is, that nine in ten of the once-awakened are now faster asleep than ever.[4]

We realize that over a period of time only a minority of those trained in these new-member meetings will come into a *koinonia* group. We accept this, remembering that leaven is a small part of the lump and recognizing that this may be one of the various ways in which the few who are chosen are distinguished from the many who are called.

Our strategy in approaching people outside the church is as follows:

1. Personal call by lay ministers inviting family to worship with us. Repeated calls at proper intervals to urge family to come.

2. After a family has indicated serious interest by worshiping regularly that family is strongly urged to come to the membership meetings. It is stressed that one undertakes no commitment to join the church by attending the meetings.

3. During the course of the training meetings we do our best to present the gospel in its full dimension of judgment and grace. We are willing to lose some if it is necessary in the honest presentation of discipleship in its New Testament scope. We try to challenge the people to become living and growing disciples of Christ at the point of membership, which may then in fact be the outer sign of inner commitment to Christ.

4. Our hope and prayer are that many will be moved to come into a *koinonia* group, as the most adequate single way of assuring their continuing growth toward maturity in Christ.

It is clear to us that we are only on the verge of learning how to prepare people for membership in the church. The years immediately ahead are bound to bring about significant changes throughout the church in the matter of membership. There is already widespread reappraisal of the current standards of membership and procedures for taking in and removing persons from the membership roll. These standards and procedures must be reformed and refitted to expedite a status of membership which in truth can be the outer symbol of inner personal commitment to Jesus Christ, with all its implications for the lay ministry in church and world.

A by-product of these training meetings has been the growth of the lay leaders themselves. Our lay ministers grow more through the sharing of their faith in these meetings than in any other way. Here is the statement of a woman who, together with her husband, was awakened in a *koinonia* group; she began to take up her ministry, and was powerfully used by God in the training of new members:

I began to read *The Experiment of Faith* as preparation for my training. The sentence about accepting as much of Christ as you are able to understand with as much faith as you now possess—seemed to jump out at me. There I was, teaching Sunday School, leading new members in discussions on prayer, witness, etc., and I hadn't made any commitment to Christ myself. So I knelt down and prayed, and for the first time committed myself to God, asking for grace to fulfill that commitment.

And opportunity wasn't long in coming. One of the new members called me on the telephone about a particular problem she had, and I suggested she pray about it and I would too. She thanked me for it and later said her prayers had been answered. I felt God had used even me to accomplish His purpose, and it was a very meaningful and humbling experience.

This is conscious discipleship. It is significant that this woman's opportunity to minister came after she understood her call to minister and opened herself to God to be used. A great breakthrough comes when one consciously takes up his ministry. This is the priesthood of all believers in action, when the people begin to minister each to the other. This is the time when disciples grow into apostles.

Koinonia known in the church becomes *koinonia* shared in the world. The lay ministry emerges in the church, and the church begins to be leaven in the world. Slowly the church becomes God's new creation, and recovers her mission to the world.

XII

The Recovery of Mission

> . . . and you shall be my witness in Jerusalem . . .
> and to the end of the earth.
>
> Acts 1:8

The recovery of mission comes slowly and imperceptibly. It doesn't come by programs or rallies or crusades. The recovery of mission always centers in the person. The person who is converted to his share in the new creation takes up his ministry and recovers his mission. The one who has been living the old life of nominal church membership or of paganism is awakened to the new life of discipleship. He comes to himself; he is found; he remembers or discovers for the first time who he is. As it is written in First Peter, "You are a chosen race, a royal priesthood, a holy nation, God's own people, that you may declare the wonderful deeds of him who called you out of darkness into his marvelous light" (I Peter 2:9). This new disciple of Christ becomes aware that he is a part of a holy nation, a community which is different from all other communities, a community in which Christ is the difference. As he begins to live his discipleship, he discovers that he is in fellowship with a royal priesthood, a priesthood of believers in which each ministers to the other. He takes up this priesthood, this lay ministry. As he takes up his ministry in the church and in the world, he finds that he has indeed been chosen, chosen for special mission. He feels a compulsion to serve and witness, a divine compulsion. He knows that God has laid His hand upon him. He hears the words spoken to him, "You did not choose me, but I chose you and appointed you that you should go and bear fruit . . ." (John 15:16). And he cannot keep himself from responding, "Here am I, Lord. Send me." So the disciple of Christ becomes an apostle for Christ. A learner in the church is sent into the world "to declare the wonderful deeds."

The recovery of mission centers in the person and only with time becomes effective in the church. As the lay ministers become leaders in the church, as the leaven works in the lump, quietly and gradually the church may recover its mission. From the outside all may appear to be the same as ever. But on the inside there is ferment; there is rising concern, a dissatisfaction with what the church has been doing, an awareness that the church has mistaken her mission or has failed to fulfill it. There is a sense of urgency, a new dependence upon God, a willingness to experiment. A people who discover that they are chosen, a royal priesthood, a holy nation, are at the threshold of recovering their mission. First comes the awareness of who we are; then the conviction of what we should be doing. Our faltering steps toward the recovery of our mission at Aldersgate Church may now be indicated.

There is recovery of mission within the church. Many church members are discovering the reality of loving and being loved in Christ, the fulfilling of Jesus' commandment, "This is my commandment, that you love one another as I have loved you" (John 15:12). There is evidence of a rising compassion for fellow members who are shut-in, sick, hospitalized, in trouble, or even in financial distress. For some time a Visitation Committee has been responsible for taking flowers to shut-ins, sending cards to sick persons, etc. Not long ago, a woman returned from the hospital to spend several days confined to her home. She became depressed. A friend in her *koinonia* group came to see her, brought her a dozen roses, and more important, brought her Christ's love in person. The convalescing woman telephoned me, told me the incident, and said that this call had meant so much to her she wanted to begin calling on others in the same way. So, quite informally, she took up this compassionate ministry to hospitalized and sick members of the church.

One morning in a sermon I mentioned what this woman was doing and asked any persons who were interested in this kind of ministry to speak to me. The response was amazing. I discovered that a veritable well of compassion existed which had only been waiting to be tapped. Approximately twenty-five persons said they wanted to take up this ministry. I am now working with them, informing them when people are hospitalized, sending them to visit the sick, shut-ins, those in hospitals, new mothers, and in some instances bereaved families. Beyond this formal recruitment of lay pastors, informal visitation has risen considerably. Often when I call on a church member in the hospital, I will find that another church member has been there, has come entirely on his own initiative simply out of loving concern for fellow church members. People naturally are most inclined to call upon church members they know, but many are also calling on complete strangers within the church. The church is slowly becoming the Body of Christ in which we are individually members one of another (Romans 12:5).

A more tangible expression of the same mutual love occurred recently in the area of finance. By way of background it may be said that the giving level within the church has increased four times while the membership has doubled. Two new buildings have been built, with the result that one-third of our annual budget must go to debt retirement. In this context of real and continuing need for money for institutional, pastoral, and mission work, we have recovered our mission of unconditional liability, even financial liability, for each other. Here is what has happened. Several years ago there was a recession in which some church families were in financial straits. At that time voluntary contributions resulted in approjximately $350.00 for the distressed families. Recently a church family found itself in an emergency situation. The father had been suffering mental illness for several years. The time came during a particular confinement when his hospitalization insurance was exhausted. He was forced to move to a State Hospital where the charge was nineteen dollars a day. So this family, supported by the moderate earnings of the wife, found itself going into debt at the rate of nineteen dollars a day. Several church members were greatly concerned. One man finally took action. He began telephoning church members and asking them to give enough to support the sick man for one day or more. Over a period of several weeks, $715.00 was raised for his family. The immediate emergency was at least partly met.

However, this experience caused many to believe that the church as a corporate fellowship should give some expression of concern and responsibility in such a situation. It was good that individual church families should voluntarily come to the aid of a distressed family, but it would be even better for mutual liability in love to be expressed tangibly and specifically in the church budget. A proposal came to the Official Board from the Commission on the Mission of the Church recommending that one thousand dollars be set aside in the annual budget for the aid of any church family suffering emergency financial distress. It was suggested that this fund be administered by a special committee consisting of the minister, lay leader, chairman of the Commission on the Mission of the Church, president of the Woman's Society, and president of the Men's Fellowship. It was further suggested that no more than five hundred dollars should be kept in this fund at the end of any fiscal year, in order that every year this item should appear in the annual budget to remind us of our mutual loving liability for one another.

There was considerable discussion. It was pointed out that precedent for financial liability existed in the early church. Luke writes in Acts, "Now the company of those who believed were of one heart and soul, and no one said that any of the things which he possessed was his own, but they had everything in common. . . . There was not a needy person among them. . . and distribution was made to each as any had need" (Acts 4:32–35). When the vote was taken, overwhelming approval was given to the proposal. The fact that our concern for one another is built into our annual budget stands as a powerful symbol of the solidarity of those who seek to love one another as Christ has loved us.

There is recovery of mission to other churches. We are recognizing our obligation to go and witness in other churches. One winter a group of our men went on a retreat, as previously related. The following spring a request came from a church in our city asking us to send someone to tell their men's group about our retreat. Three of our men went. It happened that all three men were in a prayer group together. In the course of describing the nature of the retreat weekend, they told something of their prayer group and the men's group in our church. One of them said: "In our men's group we don't go much for raising money, and projects of that sort. We try to spend our time together in ways that will encourage our spiritual growth. We ask other laymen to come and share their religious experience and concern with us." This man didn't know that the men's group to which he was speaking had spent much of its energy that year in just such money-raising projects, with very little time or energy left for encouraging their own spiritual growth. The effects of this witness were powerful. The leaders of the men's group began to reconsider the purpose of their organization. Some of the men went on a retreat weekend. A few of them came back determined to start a prayer group. This prayer group became a center of new life in that church.

Opportunities are limitless for this kind of lay witness in other churches. As we have been helped by laymen coming to help us, so we are sending our lay ministers to help elsewhere. One of our men preached on a Layman's Sunday in a church located some distance from Cleveland, sharing our experience with small groups. One of our women led a retreat for the women of another church. We recognize the fact that laymen are impressed and powerfully moved by the witness of other laymen. Lay witness clearly is the predominant feature of the recovery of mission.

The recovery of mission grows and expands when converted persons move to new communities and join other churches. A couple, awakened and growing in a *koinonia* group, moved away from Cleveland. At the time of their departure they wrote: "We are leaving Aldersgate with regrets, but looking forward to a new future in Arizona—to be apostles as well as disciples, because I feel you are surely sending us with a mission. I pray that we can help to accomplish even a little of what you expect of us." That husband and wife go as apostles for Christ into a new place, a new future, a fortunate new church. They go expecting to be used by God. They know that they are on mission. Recently a letter came from the minister of a church to which another converted couple had gone. The minister writes, "I am deeply grateful that the Smiths are about to become members of this church. You will be interested to know that they have been instrumental in starting a discussion group in this parish. Their experience with a similar group at Aldersgate made then enthusiastic about beginning one here. Their excellent spirit, their willingness to work, and their concern for matters of vital importance stem in part, I am sure, from their experience at Aldersgate."

We are discovering that the mobility of American life, which makes the task of reaching people difficult, facilitates the sending into other places of those who have been reached. Persons who have become apostles are transferred by secular agencies to take up their apostleship in new and different places. So the Holy Spirit blows the seeds here and there, always onto new ground. Mobility makes for maximum opportunity. The local church must infect its people with the germ of *koinonia*, so that wherever they go they will infect others, and the contagious new life in Christ will spread. The local church, which fears to lose its life as some of its lay ministers move away, discovers that it must lose its life. But in losing its life, the local church saves its life. For in order to maintain the ministry in the local church as some of the veteran lay ministers leave, the pressure is always upon us to awaken and train new people for their ministry. This means that we must constantly be engaged in leading people into the event of conversion. We must nurture them in the climate of *koinonia* as they become sharers in the new creation, guide them as they take up their ministry, and pray for them as they discover their mission in the world.

There is recovery of mission in daily work. Most men find it almost impossible to relate their Christian faith to their daily work in any redemptive way. A member of our church who is a psychologist in a management-consultant firm and whose own work is counseling with other men about their problems at work, says that most men check their religion at the door when they come to their daily job. Yet, the lay ministers are beginning to act as salt, light, and leaven where they work. They believe that first they must do the best job they can at their particular occupation. They must treat other people on the job with Christian love. Then they must be alert to the opportunities to serve and witness. Conversation on the job at coffee breaks and lunch hours, and en route to and from work provides many opportunities. Moral issues which are current on the local and national and international scene naturally arise, providing chances to affirm one's Christian convictions. A salesman described an interview with a customer in which he was asked to arrange a business meeting on a particular weekend. He replied that he couldn't because he was going on a retreat that weekend. It happened that his customer was the leader of a men's group in another church, and the eventual result of this chance witness was that the men of that church went on a retreat. This same salesman prays before and during his business interviews, asking not that God should close the deal for him, but that God should bless him and the other persons and bring forth whatever is His good will from it. His daily work is carried on under the leading of prayer and with the motivation of mission.

A woman who works as a secretary commented on a particular issue to her boss. He said to her, "Did you get that idea from the funny little church you go to?" For fifteen minutes she was irritated and said nothing. Then she regained her composure and said to her boss, "I'm glad my funny little church shows." Our witness will not always be favorably received. It takes courage to be unashamed of the gospel, knowing that it is the power of God for salvation to those who accept it (Romans 1:16). We are the fellowship of the unashamed, the unapologetic; we are the witnessing community.

A man moved away from Cleveland to take another job. He wrote his minister:

Pray about my job. I need guidance and help. I have the responsibility of supervising an office that involves quite a few fellow humans. A real chance to bring Christianity to the office, though I'm still not certain that I'll be a better manager for being a Christian. Put me on your prayer list for a few weeks. Don't misunderstand me, I'm not lacking in confidence. I've asked for this chance, and if anything, I'm too sure of myself. What I need is an open heart and mind and leading that I may walk in God's way.

Here is a man honestly on mission in his job. He is trying to let his working hours be a vehicle for the work of God. He is accepting his call to be a servant of Christ and a witness for Christ in his place of work. He doesn't know exactly how Christ would use him; he doesn't have pat answers for the fulfillment of his mission; he doesn't have it all figured out. But he is willing to be used and eager to be used. Many men and women are recovering their mission in daily work.

There is recovery of mission in the neighborhood. A woman related recently her struggle with herself to go to the house of a neighbor whose husband had just died. She didn't want to go, would much rather have sent a note or flowers. But she felt she ought to go. She went without a knowledge of what to say but with a willingness to share both the sorrow of her neighbor and her own faith in Christ. She listened to the sadness of her neighbor; she sat with her in her broken world; she prayed with her. Unwittingly she was sharing Christ's mission to those who mourn (Matthew 5:4). For this is what it means to weep with those who weep and rejoice with those who rejoice. It is to share the depths and the heights of life with others in the presence of Christ. Many are now discovering a mission to lonely, bitter, insecure people in their own neighborhoods.

A woman of our church was talking with her neighbor. The neighbor wasn't certain whether she and her family should move out of the community or stay where they were. The woman on mission said to her, "Why don't you take it upstairs? Pray about it." The neighbor gasped in amazement and said, "Nancy! I never expected to hear anything like that from you!" The two women began talking about Christian faith and prayer. A new and deeper friendship, friendship in Christ, became real for them, because one of them had recovered her sense of mission. Many are now sensitive to times and circumstances in which they may serve and witness in the neighborhood.

There is recovery of mission in the family. Husbands and wives are discovering that they are to be ministers to each other. Some marriages are being re-created. A woman wrote recently:

Before my husband and I came to the Church we were near the separation point. Things were very dark indeed. I was and am still the one who is unable to fully and deeply express my love and concern for those dearest to me. Everyone has advice, parents, friends, relatives, books, etc., but my real need wasn't advice so much as understanding. I was smart enough to know something was wrong; however, I was pretty sure it wasn't I. It was at this time that we joined a Bible Study Group. It's impossible to fully describe the changes that took place in me in our Study Group. I entered the group so sure of my own "self-reliance"; then, somehow, very gradually without my realizing it I accepted Christ in *all* of life. Now that I had experienced the love of Christ in a small group I knew such a love must be possible between a husband and wife. I cannot now accept anything less than this forgiving and redeeming love in my marriage. I feel the responsibility is mine to create and maintain a home filled with love and a willingness to share and to accept each other as we are.

Those who are in *koinonia* groups find themselves sharing their doubts and beliefs, often for the first time. Many have begun to pray together. One salesman and his wife use the same devotional material. When he is on the road they are united in spirit through their reading and prayer. The context for forgiveness is thus sustained and renewed as hearts and minds are open to Christ. Deeper levels of understanding and compassion are known. Each begins to minister to the other.

Some marriages are coming alive with a sense of mutual mission. A man related recently that he used to think himself superior to his wife, superior in mind and ability, superior as a person. He said that in the last several years he has come to realize that in fact she is far above him as a Christian. He told some of us that he went home the other day to find that she had given fifty dollars to a neighbor family that was unable to meet a house payment. He said, "Two years ago I would have been furious with her. In this instance, we talked it over and agreed that we wouldn't expect to get the money back." Here is a couple growing in the knowledge and love of God together and taking up their mission together.

Parents are beginning to understand that they are the chief Christian educators of their children. Those who are growing in faith themselves are now able to help their children grow in faith. The traditional but highly significant practices of family grace and family devotions are being revived or taken up for the first time. A woman told a group not long ago of a mistake her five-year-old child makes in a memorized evening prayer. The prayer is supposed to go like this: "Now the light has gone away; Savior, listen while I pray." The child prays it this way: "Now the light has gone away; my Savior listens while I pray." There isn't any question about the Saviour listening while he prays. He knows his Savior listens! How does he know? Because he can see and sense that his parents know and believe. I know that home to be a home of deep and contagious Christian faith. I know that little mistake is an outward indication of the real truth that this child is receiving the gift of faith from Christ through his parents. Many parents are taking up their ministry to their children, seeking to love them as they have been loved by Christ. In the future, the church must seek to train husbands and wives for their ministries to each other and to their children.

There is recovery of mission in the community. We are seeking to make our witness more effective in our own community. We discover that being witnesses in "Jerusalem" is far more difficult than being "witnesses to the end of the earth." Most church members will agree that we must send money to mission stations at home and abroad. Most local churches will fulfill the denominational apportionments for missionary work and will gradually give above and beyond these obligations, as they are able. The church member is willing to send his money partly because he knows that he will not be personally involved in this mission to the end of the earth. But when we draw the circle of mission more narrowly and speak of the whole city of "Jerusalem," or Cleveland, as our obligation, the going gets harder. People in a suburban church do not want to be reminded of their obligation to the city. They work in the city by day, but flee the city by night. They do not want to regard the whole city as their necessary concern. Yet we know that the politics and housing and race problems of the city are the legitimate concerns of any suburban church which would recover its mission.

But we really run into trouble when we underline the circle of mission responsibility around our local community. There the probability of involvement is great. A local church simply cannot avoid the finger of responsibility when it considers its own community, for there it clearly is the people of God through whom He would work. If we are really to be the Body of Christ in our local community in the area of politics, housing, or race relations, we will have to take stands and begin to do something. We of Aldersgate Church were confronted with a situation which suddenly and clearly crystallized our own local mission. It had to do with the problem of race relations in greater Cleveland. It was one of those events which no one anticipated, which caught us all by surprise. In retrospect, I believe it was the leading of the Holy Spirit. In order to get a clear picture of this event, a brief background in the race-relations history of our church may be useful.

I began serving this church in the summer of 1954, the year in which the Supreme Court decision on segregation in the schools was made. This decision brought to public attention the most important domestic social problem in twentieth-century America. In the years that followed, sermons were regularly given in our church on the Christian faith and the race problem. Negro preachers and speakers were invited to speak at Lenten services. In 1957, we exchanged ministers and choirs with a Negro church one Sunday. This was the first of such exchanges which have become an annual fellowship. The last two years some of the people of both churches have shared in the exchange. There were annual exchanges of fellowship in our Senior High Youth Group and in our Woman's Society. In 1958, the Official Board declared itself on record that there was no color bar to membership in Aldersgate Church. Since there were no Negroes in our community, this decision had no immediate effect. In 1959, the Education Commission of the Church presented a statement to the Official Board concerning Aldersgate's responsibility to prepare its people for the time when a Negro family or families would be within the area of our natural parish responsibility. Recommendations for ways and means of further preparation included the use of Negro music from time to time by choir and congregation in morning worship, the hiring of a Negro assistant pastor for the summer months, the invitation to some Negroes to share in our Vacation Church School, the suggestion that study groups within the church devote a meeting or meetings to the discussion of the matter, and the suggestion that those who have Negro friends invite them to worship with us occasionally. It was pointed out that none of these recommendations was new or unusual, all having been carried out by urban and suburban churches in other communities. This report was received with raised eyebrows, little comment or discussion, and without recommendation for specific action. Some individual action was taken, however. Two families did bring Negro friends to worship with us. Those in charge of Vacation Church School began to consider how to arrange for a few Negro youngsters in the school. This resulted in tentative plans to include a Negro teacher and a few pupils in the Vacation Church School for the summer of 1960.

This, then, is the background which provides the setting for what happened in the spring of 1960. This was the time of the riots and killings in South Africa. This was the time of the sit-in counter demonstrations in the South. This was the time when the bill for Negro voting rights was being debated in Congress. So it was that I felt compelled to change the Lenten preaching plans for Palm Sunday and the preceding Sunday, and to preach on race relations and our Christian responsibility. The first sermon sketched the progress made by the Negro in the last twenty years, visible by laws and rulings made in his favor during those years. The areas of continuing discrimination were noted. The second sermon, preached on Palm Sunday, stated that some Negro families would probably move into our geographical parish community within the next decade. The time had come for us to prepare for this eventuality. The recommendations for specific action included the refusal to accept restrictive racial covenants in housing, the increase of fellowship with Negro people in all possible ways, and the possibility of an interracial Vacation Church School. It was also suggested that we speak up for justice and love when the race problem was raised in conversation at work or in the community. There was nothing very startling about these comments, and the congregational reaction was good.

Palm Sunday afternoon the Church Editor of a Cleveland newspaper telephoned me to ask what had been said in the sermon that morning. I gave him the gist of the sermon. The next morning a large article appeared in that paper under the headline, "Prepare to Integrate, Suburb Minister Says." The article took the sermon out of its Palm Sunday context and stressed the imminence of Negroes moving into our community, but was otherwise accurate. The evening paper came out with a lead, "Pastor Opens Way for Influx of Negroes," with important inaccuracies. There were reports of the sermon on the radio. Because of the climate of world and national feeling on race relations at the time, it happened that this sermon became a subject of discussion and debate for some days in the greater Cleveland area. Phone calls and letters came; most but not all of them were favorable. One anonymous telephone caller declared he was going to blow up our home. Another threatened to print handbills attacking the sermon and to distribute them outside our church the next Sunday. Of the unfavorable letters all but one were anonymous, and uniformly they were written in crude language and often with great vulgarity.

Through the week increasing encouragement came from members of the congregation. One medical student who has grown up in the church wrote: "If this controversy manages to grow to any unforeseen or unusual proportions and you get called on any carpets in regard to this stand, I would be most happy to stand with you, if you find you could use my little bit of help." A man who had only recently become a member of the church wrote: "I would like to take this opportunity to offer you my complete support. . . . The time has certainly come when Christians must begin to collect the scattered pieces of this race problem and re-assemble them the way the Lord intended. I sincerely hope you continue to bring the word of God to the pulpit rather than the words of the community in which we both live or the word of the congregation to whom you preach." Men were being asked about the matter at work; women were being called about it in the neighborhood. Within a few days literally hundreds of our church members found themselves having to witness one way or the other. One man related how he spent an hour and a half during a lunch hour explaining his conviction about it to officers of the firm which employs him. At a *koinonia* group where the matter was discussed, two men found themselves a minority of opposition to the stand of the sermon. One of them said in real humility to the other, "I guess we'll have to help each other grow in understanding."

Not all the reactions were favorable, by any means. Some women called the Director of the Vacation Church School and said they would withdraw their children if there were any Negroes in the school. Some church leaders were worried as to the effect of the whole affair on the financial support of the church. Many thought the newspaper publicity was unfortunate. But out of those days came a strong sense of the solidarity of our Christian fellowship, a fellowship strong enough to sustain internal discussion of considerable emotional content, and strong enough to sustain outside pressures of many kinds. Only once did anyone within the church say to me that I ought not to have preached these sermons. Not once did anyone question the freedom of our pulpit. One man said to me, "I don't know that I'm ready to buy the whole package. I just don't know what I would do if a Negro family bought the house next door. But my mind isn't closed, and it sure has been changing these last few years!" We discovered that many of our minds and hearts had been changing. A teacher in the community said to me, "If this thing had happened five years ago, the church would have split apart, and you might have been forced to leave." Perhaps he was right. In any case, we found that under the pressure of these events we stood together. Though there was diversity of opinion, there was unity of fellowship. We determined to continue our efforts to prepare ourselves for a time of integrated living. We discovered our own small but real recovery of mission in the community.

It will be painfully clear to the reader that we have just scratched the surface of our mission. We are still in the position of the typical local church, and have yet to fulfill our mission. Like the Prodigal Son, we have come to ourselves and now must start the long trek home. As we grope uncertainly and walk unsteadily on the edge of recovering our mission in the world, we see before us wide-ranging implications for the life of the conventional church in our time. Two of these implications are worthy of mention here.

It is necessary to re-examine the structure of the local church. Too often the existing structure of the local church is not geared to facilitate mission. Churches suffer from hardening of the institutional arteries. New blood is sometimes blocked; new life is sometimes stifled. We are cursed with bigness. Our programing tends toward ever larger numbers, and we know that significant personal changes seldom occur in crowds but, rather, in small groups. Much of our energy must go to keep the wheels of organizational life spinning. Our most devoted people spend their time in this apparently necessary busywork, too tired and overworked to grow in mind and spirit. As someone put it, "We are so embroiled in church work that we have no time or energy for the work of the church." We must have the courage to let *koinonia* determine and shape its own structure. We will seek to use existing organizations and groups to house *koinonia*, making whatever changes seem wise and necessary. But we will face the fact that some existing structures will remain impervious to the new life. Old soldiers may fade away, but old organizations in local churches have greater longevity than old soldiers. Some old structures in our churches may have to die, in order that new structures may come into being by the leading of the Spirit. This will not be easy, for many will prefer the old way of doing things. There will be misunderstanding and criticism, as there always is when new ways are suggested, even though these new ways be a return to the old ways of the early church. Professor William H. Lazareth gave a powerful witness for the necessity of experiment in a series of lectures to a group of church leaders. He said:

. . . the church itself must be a daring beach-head of human freedom. Instead of the musty museums which so many of our churches resemble (despite all their plush and chrome), we must practice what we preach and stand ready for continual reformation when the times and needs demand. Christ alone—in Word and Sacrament—is essential to the church. Everything else is adiaphoral and dispensable if it no longer serves a new age as a transparent vehicle of the gospel. Yet despite this, our churches are being crowded by flocks of sheeplike conformists who are yearning for institutional security instead of the adventure of Christian freedom. "Come weal or woe, the status quo" is the gospel of many lately-revived ecclesiastical ghettoes which sold their evangelical birthright for a mess of pot-bellied respectability.

. . . Let us say it quite clearly: refusal to change traditional patterns simply because they are traditional is a basic form of ecclesiastical idolatry. Now I am not advocating any kind of "itchy change" for its own sake: "good order" has always been the moderating criterion for Protestant externals, and rightly so. I am only pleading that we clearly distinguish in principle what is essential for the church from what is not, so that we know what can be thrown overboard in good conscience when the storms get rough. . . . Flexibility and experimentation should receive top priority in the church today.[1]

Let those who are willing to accept the criticisms accompanying experiment remember the nobility of their lineage. It was Jesus who spoke of new wineskins and who said to a group of church leaders, "You have a fine way of rejecting the commandment of God, in order to keep your tradition!" (Mark 7:9).

Exciting and significant experiments are being made in many

local churches in our time. Perhaps the single most remarkable experiment in congregational life in America today is the Church of the Savior in Washington, D.C. This is a church which began twelve years ago with three members. Today it has about sixty members, with an annual budget of over sixty thousand dollars. Membership is granted only after arduous training and preparation. Specific commitments to the life of discipleship are required. In this church there are no passengers; there is only the crew. All members are involved in worshiping, working, and witnessing. Every member belongs to a *koinonia* group with its own special mission. This is a church on mission in the world. But it is a church apart from the mainstream of typical Protestant church life. It is nondenominational and therefore is unencumbered by the ties and requirements of denominational affiliation. Its origin and growth have been in a setting unlike the history of the typical local church. What we must do is learn how to translate the *koinonia* which lives so powerfully in the Church of the Savior into the setting of the conventional local church. And we must be willing to modify the structure and organization of the local church where it seems the only way to facilitate mission.

We at Aldersgate Church have made a small beginning in the direction of such experiment by changing the name of the Commission which deals with mission from the Commission on Missions to the Commission on the Mission of the Church. The change in name is the outer sign of a concern for the church's recovery of its whole mission. This Commission is now regarding its role as seeking to understand what the church's total mission is, and how it can be expedited through the existing structure of the church. The structure for mission is usually present. The typical local church is organized for work such as that of education, finance, and evangelism. These committees are generally involved in the details and techniques of their responsibility, seldom engaging in the study and discussion and prayer which could make them vehicles for Christian mission. But this Commission is making a study of the organizational life of our church, raising questions about the purposes of organizations and committees to determine whether they facilitate or stultify the real mission of the church. It is hoped that useful changes will be made in line with the recommendations of this study. It is true of institutions as well as of persons that the old passes away and the new comes when we enter into the new creation.

It is necessary to re-examine the role of the clergyman in the local church. The typical clergyman in an urban setting is expected to go here and there, touching multitudes of persons and situations, but touching them lightly and casually. He is the executive of an organization, the defender of an institution, the promoter of a program. He becomes a public-relations man. The larger the church he serves, the more remote he becomes from his people, and the less chance there is for deep and intimate fellowship with them. The more outwardly successful the church becomes, the more its clergyman is expected to take a leading role in community responsibilities. The increasing pressure upon the clergyman is to scatter his energies in many directions, dividing his attention, diverting his purpose, and sometimes destroying his sense of mission. Samuel Miller recently described the clergyman's plight:

> One of the tragedies of our time is that the minister is both overworked and unemployed. Overworked in a multitude of tasks that do not have the slightest connection with religion, and unemployed in the exacting labors and serious concerns of maintaining a disciplined spiritual life among mature men and women. . . . Wherever the current ideal of the minister comes from—the big operator, the smart salesman, the successful tycoon—it still remains a puzzle why the minister should fall prey to such false images unless he has completely confused what he is supposed to be doing.[2]

The clergyman's abiding frustration is that in doing the many things that are useful, he may be prevented from doing the one thing needful. It is being suggested here that the one thing needful in the role of the clergyman for our time is that he prepare his people for their ministry in the church and in the world. *The chief task of the clergyman is to equip his people for their ministry.* All his work is to this end. The functions of preacher, prophet, pastor, priest, evangelist, counselor, and administrator find their proper places in the equipping ministry. The purpose of this ministry is that the people shall be trained and outfitted for their work in the church and in the world. It is difficult to find a word or term which adequately describes the equipping ministry. The term "pastoral director" certainly gives the idea of the clergyman directing other people in the fulfillment of their ministries. But in the cultural setting of our time this term too easily conjures the image of the executive behind the desk directing his subordinates by remote control. The term "manager" has the advantage of implying a continuing personal involvement of manager and those managed, but it suffers from the implication of a difference in status, authority, and responsibility between manager and managed.

A layman said to me recently, "Your job is like that of a foreman in a plant. A foreman has a twofold responsibility. First he must teach and train his men to do their work. Second, he is responsible for their production. He must watch over them, guiding and encouraging them to produce. So, you as a clergyman have to train us for our ministry, and then help us to fulfill our mission, to produce. We are called to 'go and bear fruit'; you are called to see that we do it." Without introducing yet another term to describe the role of the clergyman, we can see that he is indeed a foreman to his people. He must train his people for their ministry and work with them as they discover their mission. Typically, he must work in depth with a few persons at a time until these few become lay-foremen able to train others and thus share the ministry.

If the clergyman is truly to be the foreman to his people, his commitments and responsibilities must be tailored to this function. He must be willing to do less than he ought in other aspects of his ministry in order that he may do what he ought to fulfill his chief task. The recovery of mission for the clergyman may mean significant revision of the priorities in his daily schedule. A clergyman said in my hearing not long ago, "I don't have time to read the Bible any more." The clergyman doesn't live who can afford not to read and study the Bible. Laymen have a right to expect spiritual leadership from their clergyman. Only as clergymen beseech God in much prayer, steep themselves in the Bible, and share their growing faith with others can they themselves grow. Only as they grow can they help others grow. A first priority for the clergyman must be the deepening of his own devotional life. A second priority must be the discipline of continuing mental growth. The clergyman must be willing to study as well as to read, to dig out the ideas of creative thinkers instead of being content with the secondhand, predigested material of many magazines prepared for the clergy. A third priority is that the clergyman must be willing to deny himself the pleasures of frivolous though pleasant association in the community in order that he may have time and energy for the one thing needful. He can in fact multiply his influence on the community if he will work behind the scenes equipping his people for their ministry in the community. In addition, the clergyman must be willing to relinquish authority in some areas of the church's life. He must honestly give his people the responsibility commensurate with their ministry. He must be willing to let the lay ministers make mistakes in order that they may grow in the exercise of their ministry. The shared ministry of clergy and lay people requires shared authority and responsibility. It is not coincidental that clergy and lay people recover their mission together or not at all.

If the clergyman is to be a foreman to his people, the people must be willing to accept this relationship. They must be willing to let their clergyman spend considerable time in prayer and study. They must expect him to spend much time with small groups, training and teaching and equipping those who are becoming lay ministers. They must not expect him to appear at all of the organizational meetings in the life of the church, especially those where his presence is not necessary for training or counsel. The people must be willing to take full responsibility for much of the organizational and administrative and promotional work of the church. They must in increasing numbers take up their ministry to each other. Some must become counselors; some must become teachers; others must call on the sick and the shut-ins; others must call on the new people in the community. The people must begin to share in the pastoral work of the ministry. Only as this begins to happen can the church truly be the Body of Christ, in which we all grow up in every way into Him who is the head, into Christ.

If the clergyman is to be a foreman to his people, he must be trained for this ministry by the seminary. The seminary must help him formulate:

1. *A theology of the local church.*[3] The current reappropriation of biblical theology has appeared in the areas of Christian doctrine and Christian ethics, but only incipiently in the area of local

church life. A theology of stewardship, evangelism, education, and worship is needed. The conversation and mutual contribution of seminary teachers and practicing clergymen is necessary for the formulation of such a theology. The seminary typically separates "content" and "practical" courses, ascribing more glory to thought than to action. While this may be necessary on the whole, it is misleading in such areas of church life as those listed above. Here the divorce between purpose and procedure must be recognized, and reconciliation effected. For example, the theology and practice of evangelism should be taught by a teacher who understands the meaning of Christian evangelism and knows by personal experience its effective practice. The central course in the training of parish clergymen in a seminary might well be a course on the nature and mission of the church, in which the practical theological expression of the nature and mission of the church would be spelled out in terms of the membership and ministry (clergy and lay) of the church. It seems clear that the coming years will bring agonizing reappraisal of the meaning, conditions, and tenure of membership in the churches, and new discoveries of the scope and dimension of the ministry of the church, both clerical and lay. The seminary must equip the clergyman for the ministry of equipping the people of a local church for their ministry.

2. A theology of the clergy.[4] The seminary must co-ordinate in its own rationalization the variegated roles for which it is preparing the clergyman, in order that he may have a clear understanding of the proper relationship between his many functions and his chief task. This may mean that such matters as preaching and counseling are better taught as functions of the equipping ministry than as arts and skills to be developed and possibly used simply as isolated roles which the clergyman executes. It is not a tragedy if the graduating seminary student knows little about conducting a wedding, funeral, baptism, or official board meeting. These valuable bits of knowledge he can and will obtain soon enough in the life of the local church.

A graduating seminary student needs to know the central purpose of his ministry. Once he understands his chief purpose, then he can see how his preaching and teaching and counseling and all the other things he must do contribute to his main task. And he will then be enabled to discipline the uses of his time and energy as valid expressions of his equipping ministry.

3. *A theology of the laity.*[5] If the clergyman's chief task is to equip his people for their ministry, he must study to discover the nature of their ministry. What is the New Testament dimension of the lay ministry? Hendrik Kraemer has suggested a theological grounding for this, and now the need is to spell out just what this means in the life of a local church. How are the clergyman and the layman related in their sharing of the ministry and mission of the church? How is the average church member to be so confronted and prepared that under the leading of the Holy Spirit he may take up his ministry in fellowship with others? How ought he to be trained for the work of his particular ministry in the church, in his family, in his neighborhood and community, at his place of work? The seminary must train the student in the meaning and practice of the lay ministry in the local church and in the world.

The Holy Spirit is at work in power in our time. The dry bones are beginning to live again. The hand of God, still small on the horizon, is becoming big with judgment and renewal over us. Persons are being converted. The new creation is appearing. The lay ministry is emerging. Disciples are becoming apostles. There is hope for the recovery of mission. Now is the day of salvation. Now are Christ's people summoned to prepare for His coming. Amen. Come, Lord Jesus!

Notes

Chapter I. THE LOSS OF MISSION

1. *Cleveland Plain Dealer*, September 19, 1959, p. 12.
2. *Beyond Survival* (New York: Harper & Brothers, 1959), pp. 1, 62.
3. "The Lost Generation," *Saturday Review*, September 12, 1959, p. 13.
4. From a lecture, "Priesthood Not Priestcraft," presented at the Joint Assembly of the Divisions of Home and Foreign Missions, National Council of the Churches of Christ in the U.S.A., December, 1959.

Chapter II. THE NECESSITY OF CONVERSION

1. Erik Routley, *The Gift of Conversion* (Philadelphia: Muhlenberg Press, 1955), p. 30.
2. *New York Times Magazine*, May 6, 1956, p. 22.
3. *They Gathered at the River* (Boston: Little, Brown and Co., 1958), p. 26.

Chapter III. CONVERSION BEGINS IN AWAKENING

1. *The Christian Idea of Education* (New Haven: Yale University Press, 1957), p. 15.
2. Elizabeth Burns, *The Late Liz* (New York: Appleton-Century-Crofts, 1957), pp. 172 ff.
3. *Witness* (New York: Random House, 1952), p. 16.

Chapter IV. CONVERSION CONTINUES BY DECISION

1. "Meditations in an Empty Room," *Our Times: The Best from the Reporter Magazine*, ed. by Max Ascoli (New York: Farrar, Straus and Cudahy, 1960), p. 501.
2. Act III, Scene 3.
3. *Christianity and Crisis*, April 2, 1956.

Chapter V. CONVERSION MATURES BY GROWTH

1. Wyon, *On the Way* (Philadelphia: Westminster Press, 1958), pp. 35–36.
2. *Ibid.*, pp. 62–63.

Chapter VI. CONVERSION ENDURES IN DISCIPLINE

1. Quoted by Allen Drury, *Cleveland Plain Dealer*, January, 19, 1959, p. 12.

2. *Witness*, pp. 286, 278.

3. *Ibid.*, pp. 211, 342.

4. P. L. Parker (ed.), *John Wesley's Journal* (London: Isbister and Co., 1902), p. 124.

5. F. A. Norwood, *Church Membership in the Methodist Tradition* (Nashville: Methodist Publishing House, 1958), chap. iv, p. 98.

6. N. Curnock (ed.), *Journal* (London: The Epworth Press, 1958), Vol. III, p. 285.

Chapter VII. CONVERSION TAKES PLACE IN KOINONIA

1. *The Conduct of Life* (New York: Harcourt, Brace and Co., 1951), p. 276.

2. Samuel Emerick (ed.), *Spiritual Renewal for Methodism* (Nashville: Methodist Evangelistic Materials, 1958), p. 16.

3. *Ibid.*, p. 17.

4. *Ibid.*, p. 25.

5. "On a Moment of Triumph," *Saturday Review*, May 30, 1959, p. 24.

Chapter VIII. THE IMPERATIVE: CONVERSION WITHIN THE CHURCH

1. Title taken from Elton Trueblood, *The Yoke of Christ* (New York: Harper & Brothers, 1958). See sermon, "Conversion within the Church," p. 50.

2. New York: Dodd, Mead and Co., 1955, p. 131.

3. William H. Whyte, *The Organization Man* (Garden City. N.Y.: Doubleday-Anchor Books, 1957), p. 418.

4. *Life* magazine, October 6, 1958, p. 59.

Chapter IX. THE STRATEGY: KOINONIA GROUPS

1. London: Mowbray Press, 1956.

2. New York: Harper & Brothers, 1953.

3. New York: Association Press, 1957.

4. New York: Harper & Brothers, 1954.

5. Philadelphia: Westminster Press, 1955.

6. Greenwich, Conn.: Seabury Press, 1950.

7. Philadelphia: Westminster Press, 1954.

8. Philadelphia: Westminster Press, 1958.

9. Philadelphia: Westminster Press, 1956.

10. Greenwich, Conn.: Seabury Press, 1951.

11. Melbourne: Spectator Publishing Co., PTY Ltd., n.d.

12. Garden City, N.Y.: Doubleday and Co., 1955.

13. Philadelphia: Westminster Press, 1957.

14. Nashville: Abingdon Press, 1951–1957.

15. New York: Harper & Brothers, 1928.

Chapter XI. NEW CREATION IN THE CHURCH: THE LAY MINISTRY EMERGES

1. Robert McAfee Brown, *The Significance of the Church* (Philadelphia: Westminster Press, 1956).

2. Samuel Shoemaker, *The Experiment of Faith* (New York: Harper & Brothers, 1957).

3. W. E. Sangster, *Teach Us to Pray* (London: The Epworth Press, 1951).

4. P. L. Parker (ed.), *John Wesley's Journal*, p. 298.

Chapter XII. THE RECOVERY OF MISSION

1. From a lecture, "The Church's Faithful Inreach," presented at the Joint Assembly of the Divisions of Home and Foreign Missions, National Council of Churches of Christ in the U.S.A., December, 1959.

2. "The Evaluation of Religion," *Saturday Review*, November 14, 1959, p. 70.

3. T. A. Kantonen, *Theology of Evangelism* (Philadelphia: Muhlenberg Press, 1954); *A Theology for Christian Stewardship* (Philadelphia: Muhlenberg Press, 1956).

4. David J. Ernsberger, *A Philosophy of Adult Christian Education* (Philadelphia: Westminster Press, 1959), chaps. i, ii, iii.

5. Hendrik Kraemer, *A Theology of the Laity* (Philadelphia: Westminster Press, 1958). This contains excellent study material for clergymen.

INDEX

Abraham, 55
Adam, 25, 37
Alcoholics Anonymous, 33
Aldersgate Church (Cleveland, O.), 21 passim
Allan, Tom, 79
Andrew, St., 39
Augustine, St., 81

Baptism, 109
Barclay, William, 86
Bardot, Brigitte, 40
Benedict, Donald, 98
Berrill, N. J., 73
Bible
    King James version, 21
    neglect of theology of, 81
    Revised Standard Version, 13, 22
    study of, 60–61, 83
    see also Gospels; New Testament
Bible Speaks to You, The, 86
Bible Study Groups, 22 passim
    outline for first six meetings, 111–120
    suggestions for, 98–101
    see also Koinonia groups
Brown, Mrs. Herman, 10
Brown, Robert MacAfee, 86
Burns, Elizabeth, 33
Buttrick, George, 87

Carr, John Lynn, 9
Casteel, John, 79
Chambers, Whittaker, 34–35, 57
Character, Christian, 26
Christianity
    automatic pilot theory, 47
    contemporary, 25
Church
    conversion within, 73–77

local, theology of, 143
and loss of sense of mission, 14–15
modern, 24–25
new creation in, 88–102
re-examination of structure of, 138
and worldly status and power, 16–17
Church of the Savior (Washington, D.C.), 140
Clergyman
    role of, in local church, 141–145
    theology of, 144
Commitment, quality of, 58
Communion, 68, 85
Communism, 57–58
Consider the Bible, 86
Conversion
    and awakening, 31
    continued by decision, 38–46
    in the church, 73–77
    matured by growth, 47–54
    necessity of, 20
Corporate worship, 59, 93
Cosby, Gordon, 9
Cousins, Norman, 71

Discipline, 56
    group, 99–100
Doctrine, Christian, 83, 84–85
Doing the Truth, 87

Education, and loss of mission, 14
Edwards, Jonathan, 81
Eliot, T. S., 13
Evangelical Lay Academies, 79
Evangelism, 144
Experiment of Faith, 114, 117, 122, 124

Face of My Parish, The, 79

151

Fadiman, Clifford, 14
Faith of the Church, 87
Faith of the Gospel, The, 87
Fellowship
  Christian, 89–91, 96
  monastic, 79
Finances, church, 127–128
Fosdick, Harry Emerson, 48
Freer, H. W., and Hall, F. B., 79
Freud, Sigmund, 22
Fuller, Edmund, 31

Gideon, 55
God
  awakening to, 34
  concepts of, 92
  working of, 28
Golden, Harry, 75
Gospel of Mark, The, 86
Gospels, 84–87
Grace, 31
  grooves of, 59–63
  healing, 34
  mystery of, 32
Graham, Billy, 41, 42, 74

Hamlet, 43–44
Holy Spirit, 28, 39, 58, 66, 76–77,
    80, 102, 130, 134–135
  and conversion, 32
Horse's Mouth, The, 31
House-church movement, 79

Interpreter's Bible, The, 86, 87

James, St., 39
Jesus Christ, 23–24, 27, 28–29, 55,
    109–110
  decision for, 44–45
  personal commitment to, 40, 41
John, St., 89
John of the Cross, St., 50
Johnson, Robert, 86
Joseph of Arimathea, 25

Kazin, Alfred, 22
Kee, Howard, 87
Khrushchev, 13
Koinonia groups, 36–37, 45–46, 64,
    67
  conversion in, 65–72

results, 88
strategy, 78–87
Kraemer, Hendrik, 145

Laity, theology of, 145
Late Liz, The, 32
Lay ministry, 64, 97, 126, 130
  and call to preach, 106
  emergence of, 103–124
  as leaders in church, 104
Laymen's Theological Library, 86
Lazareth, William H., 16
Lippmann, Walter, 13–14
Luckey, Charles, 9
Luther, Martin, 81, 113

Making Ethical Decisions, 87
Mannes, Marya, 40
Man's Emerging Mind, 73
Matisse, Henri, 31
Meaning of Christ, 86
Mellon, Mr. and Mrs. William Lari-
    mer, Jr., 38–39
Methodists, 69–70
Michelangelo, 37
Middle age, and conversion, 28
Miller, Samuel, 141
Mission
  loss of, 13, 14
  mutual, 133
  recovery of, 125–145
    in community, 134–138
    in daily work, 130–131
    in family, 132–134
    in neighborhood, 132
    to other churches, 128–130
Mooney, Mrs. Robert, 10
Moses, 55
Mumford, Lewis, 69
Murrow, Edward R., 41
*My Commitment to Christian Dis-
    cipleship*, 120

Negroes, 135–138
Neill, Bishop Stephen, 46
Nicodemus, 23–24, 27, 28–29
Niebuhr, Reinhold, 42
New Testament, 18, 25
  and justification by faith, 23

On the Way, 49

Osborn, Eric, 87

Packard, Vance, 32
Paderewski, 60
Parables of Jesus, 87
Parish Comes Alive, The, 79
Paul, St., 18, 48, 50, 56, 79, 82, 88, 112
Pentecost, 29, 76
Peter, St., 39
Phillips, J. B., 86, 87
Pike, James, 87
Pittenger, Norman, 87
Prayers, 95, 115
    daily, 60, 75
Prodigal Son, 33–34, 43
Protestantism, liberal, 26–27, 56–57

Race relations, 134
Reformation, 81
Retreats, 81, 100–101, 131
Revivalists, 29–30
Roman Catholicism, 57

Samson, 55
Saturday Review, 14
Schubert, Paul, 9
Schweitzer, Albert, 38, 72
Secularism, 76
Seminary, 143–145
Service, 62–63
Shakespeare, William, 43

Significance of the Church, The, 86, 112, 115, 118
Sin, reality of, 25
Southcott, E. W., 79
Soviet Russia, 13–14, 17
Spiritual Renewal through Personal Groups, 79
Status Seekers, The, 32
Status seeking, 16
Stevenson, Adlai, 56

This I Believe, 41
Tithing, 21, 61, 62
Titus, 83
Trueblood, Elton, 9, 27
Two or Three Together, 79

Unitarianism, 82, 108
Upper Room, 115

Van Dusen, Henry Pitney, 42
Vocation, Protestant idea of, 63

Ways, Max, 13
Weisberger, Bernard A., 29
Wesley, John, 58, 69, 79, 102, 113, 122–123
    Journal, 58
Witness, 63–64, 88, 96
    personal, 106–107
Wyon, Olive, 49

Zacchaeus, 44

INDEX TO SCRIPTURE

OLD TESTAMENT

Ezekiel 37:1–3 13
    37:14 18

NEW TESTAMENT

Matthew 5:4 132
    5:48 53
    6:19–34 117
    18:3 .... 21, 24
    23:23 61
    25 63
    28:19 64
Mark 1:15 .... 24, 43
    7:9 139
    8:34 74
    8, 9 .... 78, 109–10
    10 .... 78, 109–10, 118
    10:17–31 117
    10:45 62–63
Luke 11:13 30
    12 112
    17:10 26
John 3:1–8 114
    3:3 .... 20, 24
    3:14 24
    13 63
    15:5 26
    15:12 126
    15:16 .... 15, 125

Acts 1:8 .... 63, 125
    2:5 112
    2:42 .... 65, 80
    2, 4 .... 117, 118
    3:19 21
Romans 1:11* 88
    1:16 131
    7:15, 18, 19, 24 50
    12:5 127
I Corinthians 3:1, 2 48
II Corinthians 1:8 51–52
    5:16–20 114
    5:17 .... 18, 24, 88
    8:3 61
    9 .... 117, 118
    13:14 65
    16 117
Galatians 5:19, 20 52
Ephesians 4:11, 12* 103
    4:14, 15, 13* 48
    4:15, 13* 47
Colossians 3:12–15 52
    3:17 53
I Timothy 4:6 82
    4:7 56
II Timothy 3:15–17* 80
Hebrews 10:24, 25 78
I Peter 1:3 24
    2:9 125
    4:17 .... 17, 73

* Phillips translation.

155